Custom Motorcycles
Choppers ▪ Bobbers ▪ Baggers

Howard Kelly

Photography by Michael Lich

D1260465

First published in 2009 by MBI Publishing Company and Motorbooks, an imprint of MBI Publishing Company, 400 First Avenue North, Suite 300, Minneapolis, MN 55401 USA

Motorbooks titles are also available at discounts in bulk quantity for industrial or sales-promotional use. For details write to Special Sales Manager at MBI Publishing Company, 400 First Avenue North, Suite 300, Minneapolis, MN 55401 USA.

To find out more about our books, visit us online at www.motorbooks.com.

Editor: Peter Schletty
Design Manager: Kou Lor
Designed by: Airbrush Action. Inc.
Cover designed by: LK Design, Inc./Laura Rades

Library of Congress Cataloging-in-Publication Data

Kelly, Howard, 1962-
   Custom motorcycles : choppers, bobbers, baggers / Howard Kelly ;
photographs, Michael Lichter.
        p. cm.
   Includes index.
   ISBN 978-0-7603-3607-6 (pbk. : alk. paper)
   1. Choppers (Motorcycles)--Pictorial works.
2. Bobbers (Motorcycles)--Pictorial works. 3. Motorcycles--Customizing I. Title.
   TL442.7.K45 2009
   629.227'5--dc22
                                    2009017855

About the author

Howard Kelly, former communications manager for S&S Cycle, has been editor at *Hot Bike* magazine and at *Street Chopper* magazine and a staff member at *Hot Rod Harleys* and *Motorcyclist* magazines. He lives in Onalaska, Wisconsin.

About the photographer

Michael Lichter's motorcycle photography has been featured in *Easyriders* magazine for over a quarter of a century. His photos have also appeared in numerous Motorbooks titles, including *Indian Larry, Choppers: Heavy Metal Art, Top Chops, Arlen Ness: Godfather of Choppers, Billy Lane Chop Fiction, Harley-Davidson Century,* and *Sturgis.* He lives in Boulder, Colorado. You can see more of his work at www.lichterphoto.com.

Printed in China

Contents

Introduction: **Bike Styles**

There are some basic names for bike styles that bring instant recognition to the biker crowd. For example, say "pro-street" to anyone who understands bikes and they picture a low-to-the-ground, modest-length bike with a big engine and a riding position that allows the rider to be ready for a drag race at any stoplight. There are always variations on the theme, but as a rule the names of different styles will hold up in a garage debate with your friends.

We covered pro-street, so let's talk about the most debated bike-style name in the world, "chopper." Originally, choppers were bikes that had as many of the stock parts "chopped" off as possible. This was an effort to lighten the bike and provide better performance, not necessarily style. But somehow, as custom bikes came into prominence,

the term transferred to the long, lean custom bikes of the 1960s. These bikes were also "chopped" in the sense that they had only as many parts as it took to get the bike down the road: no front fender—and often no front brake—certainly no turn signals, no extra luggage or body panels. Just wheels, tires, gas and oil tanks, and enough of a rear fender to hold a seat. "Chopper" became a generic term for a custom bike—and for any motorcycle to the uninformed—and debates sparked. How can a bike be a chopper when it is built from the ground up? How can a bike with extra body panels, lights, and unnecessary components be a chopper? There are no answers, but the debates are lively and fun.

"Bobber" is a term for a bike that wasn't quite chopped, but had parts cut down, or bobbed. It provided

1 Judging by the focal point of this photo, you can clearly see it's a trike. Bill Rucker added a unique homage to custom motorcycles by utilizing a regular fender on the back under the seat, rather than building a big panel to cover both tires.

a different look and stood out in comparison. Somehow the term evolved into describing a really short chopper—typically with a rigid frame, next to no additional rake or length in the frame assembly, a small gas tank mounted high on the backbone, and handlebars with a bit of lift to them. Again, open for debate, this term is used for a lot of bike descriptions.

A "trike" is, well, a bike with three wheels that doesn't have a sidecar. Not too much to that term. "Body bike" is a term used to describe bikes that seem to have all-encompassing body panels—very much the opposite of a chopper.

Last for our discussion is another term that is becoming controversial: "bagger." Originally a term used to describe a Harley-Davidson touring bike, as the custom world grew the name stuck to all custom bikes with saddlebags. Soon enough, a rigid bobber with saddlebags and a windshield could be called a bagger by some. There are a multitude of custom bikes that fall into the bagger category these days, but for the most

part we like to believe it's a term for touring bikes.

There are plenty of other bike terms for plenty of other bike styles. Space prevents a description of each, but armed with just these basic terms you should be ready to take on the rest of this book.

Once you decide what style of bike is right for you, the smaller details will follow. This book is designed to show you the multitude of looks and appearances a custom bike build can take. Divided into chapters by discrete parts and systems, the idea is that you might find inspiration from one bike's fenders, another's seat, the paint, the tanks, and on and on. Custom motorcycles should always be about the individual and never about copying someone else's look. However, taking something you admire and building on it, changing it, or improving on it . . . well, that's been the engine driving custom motorcycling since its beginning. Before you spend thousands of dollars creating a motorcycle of your own, take some time with the book that follows and plan your perfect custom build.

3

4

3 In a different approach to the trike feel, Jerry Covington used whitewall tires, hot rod wheels, and dual exhausts to give this three-wheeler a muscle car look.

4 Short and to the point, Rueben Guerra went for the full-bobber look. Notice how the rear fender was shortened to cover only as much of the tire as needed to carry a seat and taillight.

5 Shown here is another bobber version, this one showing off the importance of a small gas tank and mounting it high. Trevelen rarely leaves any question as to what style his bikes are.

6 At some point the line between chopper and pro-street started to blur, and bikes like this one built at Streamline Design showcase the look. Clearly a muscular feel, the extra rake and extended fork add attitude.

7 Old meets new, and a bobber is born. Shade Tree Fabrications used a lot of today's technology to make yesterday's designs and shapes look even cooler.

8

8 If you are going to have a touring bike, it might as well be fast. Built by Brian Klock, this bike held the title of World's Fastest Bagger. Notice how streamlined it is; it went to the Bonneville Salt Flats to get its name.

9 In his native England, riders take sportbikes and remove all the fairings and body parts to strip a bike down to its bare essence and call it a "street fighter." Russell Mitchell built his on an FXR-style frame, using only the parts necessary to get from point A to point B—some might call it a chopper, but can they really?

9

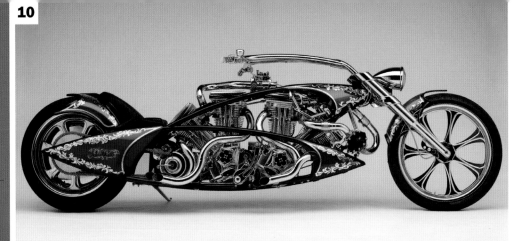

10 What do you call it when Arlen Ness puts two engines and a perimeter frame in between two tires? A radical custom that is simply cool.

11 In the case of this Donnie Smith pro-street bike, there is no question of its intent. Smith built this sleek-looking performance machine around a 145-cubic-inch engine that is capable of over 180 horsepower.

12 What the . . . ? This artistic interpretation of a board track racer was built by Chicara in Japan. It is said that he works alone in his shop and does everything by hand.

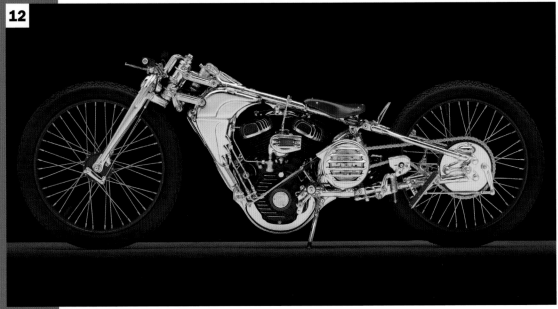

13

14

15

13 Because "chopper" isn't confusing enough, this bike is known as a "Swedish chopper." By designing the frame with very little upward or forward stretch and installing triple trees with additional rake to allow the very extended fork, the profile is an easy-to-spot design.

14 Robbie Hays built a tall chopper—that is, the frame has little to no forward stretch, but plenty of upward stretch in the downtubes. It pushes the gas tank way up in the air and adds a radical feel to the profile.

15 Combining a vintage bike style and board track racer feel, Don Hotop creates an eye-catching way to cruise down the road.

16 It's a custom . . . something. The only way to describe Mike Pugliese's bike is radically custom and cool. Friction drive, handcrafted frame, no visible lines or cables; this bike is beyond standard terminology.

17 Almost too long to fit in a single picture, Rick Fairless took the lines of an early 1970s chopper and added the engineering available today. Disc brakes, hydraulic controls, and billet wheels won't let you confuse this bike with its old inspiration, but the upgrades make it a much faster and better ride.

18 If they still raced board track today, this is the bike I would want to do it on. Russ Tom took the fundamental elements of 1920s board track racing and brought it to life in a 2000s machine resplendent with high-tech suspension, disc brakes, and plenty of power.

16
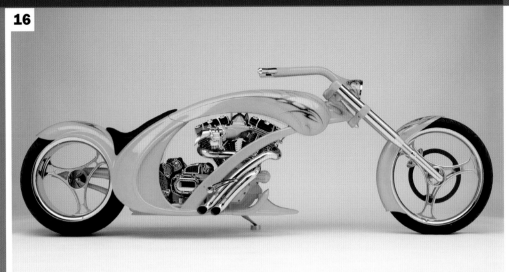

17

18

19

20

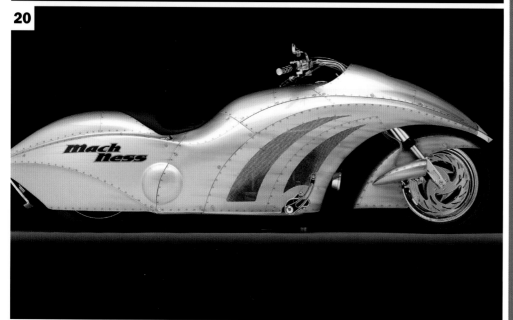

21

19 Shown here is a street fighter again, this time by Roland Sands. Born from a Harley-Davidson V-Rod, this street fighter looks to be much more fun to race around town than the original model.

20 A body bike for a reason. Underneath the metal skin lurks a turbine engine that Arlen Ness somehow came across.

21 Gangster Choppers built their interpretation of a bobber. As bare-bones as it looks, don't let it fool you. There are dozens of high-tech designs throughout the bike.

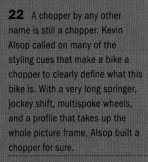

22 A chopper by any other name is still a chopper. Kevin Alsop called on many of the styling cues that make a bike a chopper to clearly define what this bike is. With a very long springer, jockey shift, multispoke wheels, and a profile that takes up the whole picture frame, Alsop built a chopper for sure.

23 Where the vision for this Chemical Choppers creation came from is beyond me. It's radical, unique, and certainly stands out in a crowd.

24 Probably the most famous body bike ever, Arlen Ness built this 1957 Chevy bike as a tribute to one of the coolest cars ever.

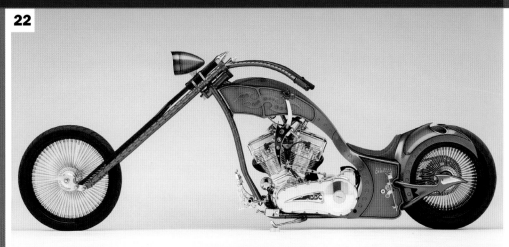

25

26

27

25 If you tried to describe Joey Perse's bike with established terminology, you would have to call it a pro-street, chopper, bagger. Or you could just call it cool and save plenty of time.

26 Aldo built a wild bike that looks ready to go drag racing or for a blast across the salt flats at a moment's notice. The AQG creation is a tribute to speed, and the massive X-Wedge engine adds a neat twist to the machine. Gas is held in the seat section and oil under the transmission—wild.

27 Marcus Walz went a few extra miles on this wild ride. It sits barely three inches above ground level, emphasizing the Ferrari theme he was going after. A single-side swingarm, frame cut-outs, and a chin spoiler are extra styling points that matter.

28 Church of Choppers brings us this hybrid chopper. Split between sportbike styling and de-raked chopper, the blend is eye catching and makes you want to blast through town slipping between cars.

29 The *Ace Café Racer* is the classic embodiment of a café racer. Designed to race around corners at a high speed, this style was the foundation for all of today's modern sportbikes.

30 This OCC machine has many styling cues that make it hard to typify. The rigid frame is complemented by a sprung seat, and the tubes stretching around the gas tank are much different than most bikes you see.

31

32

31 This is a pro-street bike. When you pull up to a traffic light and notice that the bike you are going to race has a stretched swingarm and seems to hug the ground like Skeeter Todd's bike, back out of the race gracefully.

32 Not an Indian, a Chieftan. Built by Kiwi Indian, this modern version of the classic machine is powered by a fuel-injected 56-degree V-twin.

33 Old School Chopper. Built by Chris Olson in 2008, it could have been built in 1972.

34 You could call it a chopper, or a bobber, or neither. Chopper Dave built a bike that suits his riding style by keeping the profile short, having plenty of braking power, and pulling the handlebars back to meet the mid-controls on the bike for more aggressive riding.

35 If you were looking for a way to describe the term board track racer with just one photo, this would be it. Dave Cook captured the very essence of the old race bikes in his modern homage to the style.

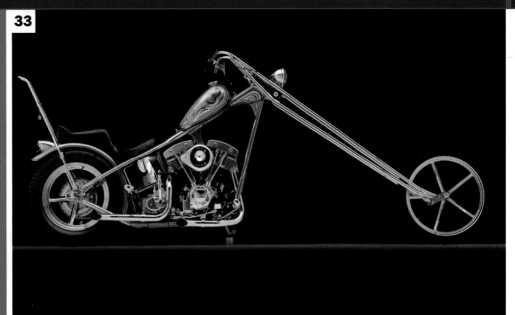

36

37

38

36 Named *Half-Day* by builder Freddie Krugger, this bike was a tribute to S&S Cycle founder George Smith and his race bike *Tramp*. Smith used to race his bike against anything anyone had. Krugger says he will do same.

37 Purposely built for land speed racing, this Bennett's Performance bike is intended to go 200 miles per hour. The fairing and tall-tail section creates an area for the rider to tuck into for high-speed aerodynamic stability.

38 I think the profile of this bike built by Jerry Covington is absolutely striking. The lines of the bike, the color choices, and the extra detail in all of the trim make it hard to look away.

39

39 Now here is a bagger that a chopper rider can love. Built by Branko, this bike combines all the best parts of his favorite bikes to be an all-around cool machine.

40 Don't know what to call Kris Krome's bike—could be a racer, could be a chopper. Whatever it is, there is nothing like it around.

41 There are many types of choppers, but this Hogtech bike is called a Swedish chopper. Not just because the shop is in Sweden, but also for the bike's style. A short rear section and a very long fork with lots of rake, accentuated by the extra rake in the trees, is the signature look for this type of bike.

40

41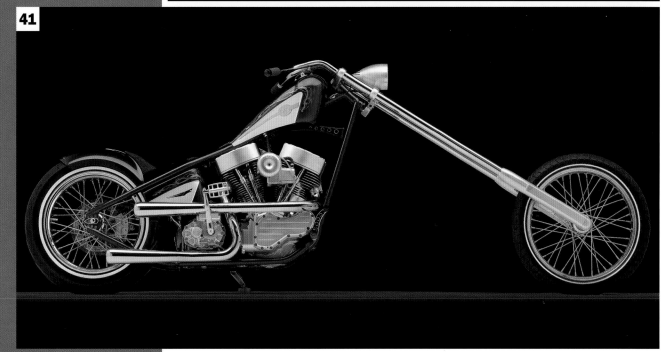

42 In my opinion this is one of the prettiest pro-street bikes I have ever seen. The subtle colors and the brilliant chrome combine to keep me looking at this bike for extended periods of time.

43 Another bagger that crosses over many boundaries. This bagger built by Zach Johnson has a 126-cubic-inch engine and routinely pulls second- and third-gear wheelies.

43

44 Fred Kodlin built this wild X-Wedge–powered bike for the S&S 50th Anniversary. To make it different, he mounted the engine backward in the bike and reversed the gearing to drive the back tire properly. The single-side swingarm and fork are over the top.

45 Now if I were building a chopper, this would be it—a pro-street chopper! A rubber-mounted engine for smoothness and rear shocks for ride comfort. Dan Roche's bike is a dream to ride.

46 Called the *Pro Tour X*, this bagger was built by Dougz Custom Paint and Fabrication. The rear bag section is one piece and lifts up and away from the rear tire to offer extra storage space like a regular saddlebag—but this looks way cooler.

1

Frames

When a group of riders get together at a local hangout to talk about their rides and their bikes, rarely do the conversations steer their way to frames. Seats, brakes, engines, carburetors . . . yes. Frames, not really so much. But in almost all bikes, the frame is the key to its look, feel, and style and how it will ride and handle.

There are three basic styles of frame in the V-twin world these days: rigid, rubber-mount, and softail. The rigid frame is the oldest design there is, basically an obtuse-angled triangle that holds everything in place. Simple, easy to work with, and really clean, the rigid frame makes a perfect platform for those with strong backs—because it is called "rigid" for a reason. Bumps will go straight through it and transfer to the rider, but it still

is cool. The softail frame *looks* like a rigid but benefits from a swing-arm connected to a pair of shocks that mount under the transmission. Unlike a car, the shocks extend when a bump is hit, so the action is not as supple as a conventional compression shock.

You get the benefit of a conventional shock and a supple ride from a rubber-mount-style frame. This design allows the swingarm to move freely with conventional shocks, and the addition of rubber-mounts for the engine and transmission eliminates almost all of the vibration transferred to the rider. (Note: the same basic frame style can be found in what is called a four-speed swingarm frame.)

A well-built frame is something worth bragging about. It is an engineering masterpiece. Older

1 Emphasizing frame stretch up and out, you see there is just enough reinforcement in the neck area to make the frame strong. Compared to the neck area, the rest of the frame looks short and compact.

2

2 With as much bodywork as there is on this Kendall Johnson machine, the frame is almost hidden. Johnson did the extensive rear section, dropped the tank low, and built up the neck area to be full and match the lines of the bike.

3 Shown here is a basic rigid frame with just a couple inches of upward stretch. No extra rake is needed when you are after this classic bobber style.

3

frames are built with 7/8-inch outer-diameter (OD) tubing, while today's frames are created with up to 2-inch OD tubing. The designer sat down and figured out how to bend it to look good and weld it together to handle your engine, potholes, and cornering forces. Frames built today also benefit from the use of CNC-cut pieces to add a higher level of precision to the axle mount, engine mounts, footpeg brackets, steering neck, and many other components.

Look closely at some custom frames and you will see designs that make you wonder how safe they can be: lengths of chain welded together to make up a section of the frame, drilled areas, and even sections that are clearly removed from the frame. But looking a little more closely will show you some innovative ideas like elliptical tubing, incorporating oil in the frame, and, of course, routing wiring through the frame for a clean look.

Still, for all this technology, few riders will brag about their frame. But it is still nice to know you have a good one.

4

5

6

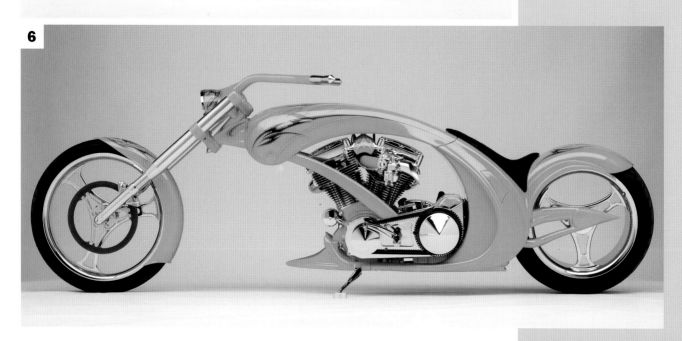

4 This classic drop-seat–style frame is built to position the rider as low as possible over the transmission.

5 At first glance this looks like a regular rigid chopper, but the extra detail really sets this frame off. Look at the steering neck reinforcement that flows into the top motor mount. Also notice that the seat tube has been repositioned behind the oil tank and transmission.

6 Again and again it will be said, "There are no rules, just the limits of your imagination." Look closely and you will see this frame has all the same elements as any other—the engine is supported, the neck braced, and the frame structurally sound.

7 Long and low, Jerry Covington's *Limo* strikes a great profile. By reversing the curve of the front downtube, the extra stretch out is almost unnoticed.

8 By putting some extra effort into the metalwork and a lot of careful paintwork, Indian Larry made his rigid frame look like it was made from bamboo.

9 Just because it is a rubber-mount-style frame, it doesn't mean the bike can't be a chopper. Arlen and Cory Ness have done a number of bikes on this frame and they are really comfortable.

10 Talk about upward stretch. This Orange County Choppers (OCC) creation has been stretched up dramatically to create a wild look. By adding no real outward stretch, the bike still looks short, even though the fork is probably 20 inches longer than stock.

7

8

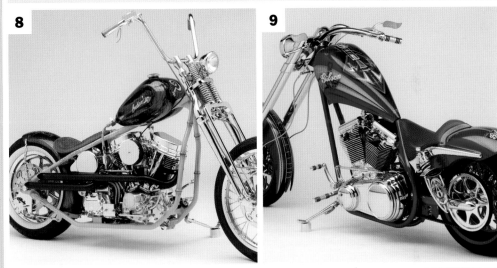

9

10

11 Sure, you could just dismiss this frame as another rigid chassis. But what would you do to account for the twisted front downtube?

12 Who says you can't customize a regular frame? This rigid frame was given twists of barbed wire and then chromed for a full custom look.

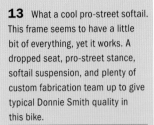

13 What a cool pro-street softail. This frame seems to have a little bit of everything, yet it works. A dropped seat, pro-street stance, softail suspension, and plenty of custom fabrication team up to give typical Donnie Smith quality in this bike.

14 Frame? Sure, it has one. How do you describe it? Simple—Arlen Ness built it to hold another of his wild creations.

15 No-nonsense, bare bones, and black. The Exile bike shown here has no frills, and has a frame that is all about business—but if you look closely you will see how incredibly clean and to the point this frame really is. It has not a single bead of weld it doesn't need, let alone brackets and tabs that shouldn't be there.

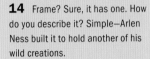

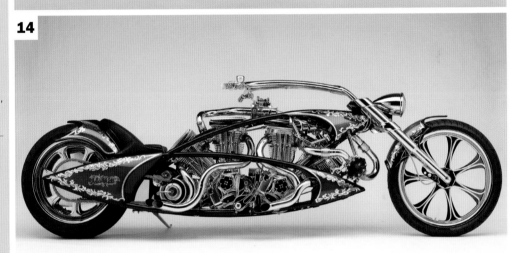

16

17

18

19

16 Shown here is a rubber-mount frame with a chopper twist. Looking very much like a traditional FXR, this bike has plenty of upward stretch to give it some personality.

17 This rigid frame features a single-loop cradle that curves around the engine in a styling tribute to board track racers of the 1920s and 1930s.

18 A stock softail frame is not a bad place to start. With some cleanup of the welds, removing the unwanted frame tabs and brackets, and adding some custom paint, this frame looks great.

19 A good look at the rear section of this frame will tell you this bike is really rigid. The extra bracing makes it look great, and the positioning of the gas tank and oil tank below the frame gives it a racier look still.

20 It's hard to see where the frame starts and the bodywork ends on Nicolas Chauvin's bike. By wrapping the body panels over frame tubes and eliminating the front downtubes, Chauvin crated a unique look that stands out in a crowd.

21 Can you say "no forward stretch but plenty of upward stretch?" This Church of Choppers rigid can.

22 Krazy Horse Customs built this wild frame that uses the engine as a stressed member. By eliminating the lower cradle, ground clearance is increased and weight is reduced. Not to mention it looks pretty racy, complementing the overall look of the bike.

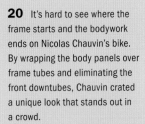

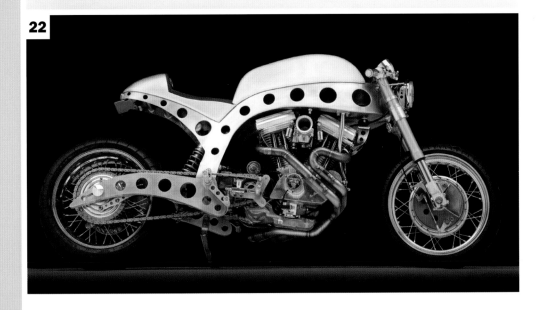

24

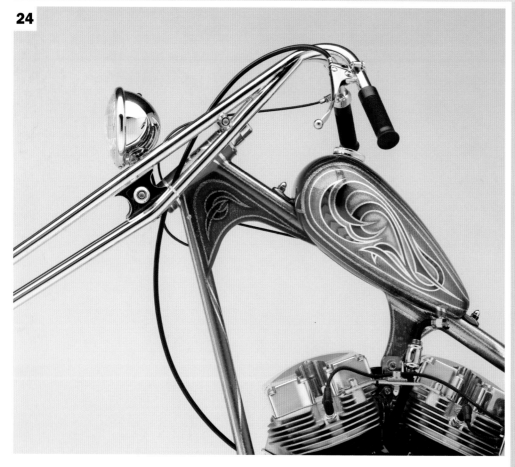

23 Kiwi Indian holds onto a retro design: the plunger suspension rigid frame. It gets a modern twist with air shocks in the back.

24 When you have this much stretch up and out, reinforcing the frame is an absolute necessity. These gusset panels offer plenty of strength and a touch of style, making room for more metalflake paint.

25 More often than not, stretch in a frame is always up or out. In the case of this racy machine built by Sucker Punch Sally, there is clearly stretch in the rear of the frame as well. The extra length adds a drag-race look to the bike.

26 Looking for a custom touch that works on any frame? Try chrome. Scott Long added a chrome frame to his bike and dressed it up far beyond what black or green would have done on this bike.

27 With the oil tank incorporated in the gas tank, the area under the seat of Chica's bike is barren. This makes it look like there is rearward stretch in the rigid frame, but it's really all in the up and out area of the neck.

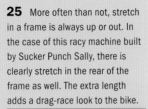

29

28 Just another racy looking rigid bike, right? Wrong. Look closely under the clutch hub, and you will see the shock and linkage to make this frame a softail style.

29 As cool little rigid frames go, this Departure Bike Works unit is right up there. Seemingly, the reinforcement usually found in the seat tube has been replaced by the solid strut-looking bars toward the rear of the bike, a nice variation on the design.

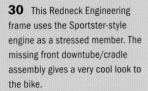

30 This Redneck Engineering frame uses the Sportster-style engine as a stressed member. The missing front downtube/cradle assembly gives a very cool look to the bike.

31 Don't dismiss this as just another rigid frame. Built by Revolution Manufacturing, this entire frame is made from carbon fiber, as are the body pieces and wheels!

32 Arlen Ness uses the frame to be the body and the gas and oil tanks of this bike. Hidden beneath the sculpted tanks is a very cool rigid chassis.

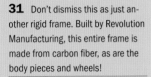

Fenders

Fenders can do a lot more than keep the rain off your back. A bike's style is often dictated by the shape and size of its fenders. Some people want big full fenders that cover the sides of the tires and some of the wheel—think Indian Chief— while others look for the smallest design possible that disappears when viewed from the side.

As you plan the bike you are building or customizing, keep in mind the bike is seen from the side most often. Think of the pictures you see in a motorcycle magazine that show the entire profile of a bike. Well, when people see you ride by, they see that same view. So what you select for fender shape will dramatically affect the stance of your bike.

In fact, while you are in the planning stages of designing your bike, try this: Locate a clear side-view picture of a bike that resembles what you plan to build. Then, start cutting fender pictures out and laying them over the picture as if you were adding fenders to the bike. You will be

2

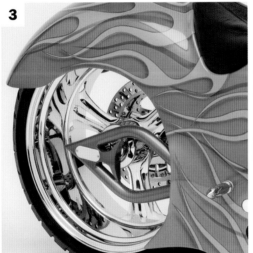

2 Laying low and almost disappearing on the tires, the fenders on this bike are as sleek as possible.

3 The rear fender of Kendall Johnson's creation does a lot. It covers the rear tire, holds the seat in place, and wraps around the battery and electronics for a clean look.

4 Rear fender? What rear fender? Joe Martin shows just what minimal really is.

amazed at how quickly the look of the bike changes.

Fenders are not limited to the traditional piece of metal that just covers a tire. Many builders use them to do double duty as a gas tank, oil tank, exhaust system, or seat pan. Some custom bikes use fenders that came from another vehicle, like a trailer or sportbike. Really, it all adds up to one simple rule: There are no rules for fenders.

OK, check that. There is one very important rule for fenders. When you decide to mount a fender low to the tire for a sleek look, be sure to allow enough clearance for the

tire to expand. Remember that tires will stretch or expand as they warm up on a ride. The faster you go, the more they expand, so one safe trick is to tape a 1/2-inch piece of rubber hose to your tire and set the fender on it before you drill the mounting holes. Most of the time this will allow enough clearance for tire expansion, but it's still best to mount the fenders before you paint them—and do a test ride to make sure.

Once you settle on a style, relax. In a few years, if you get bored with the look, you can always try something else and come up with a whole new look for your bike.

5

5 Small and to the point, this rear fender should keep some debris off the rider. But the small, light design of the fender allows for very cool fender struts to be able to support it.

6 Hugging the tire tightly and covering more than half of it, this fender really shows off Roger Goldammer's metalworking ability. The fender mounts almost disappear in the fender itself.

7 The rear fender on this OCC bike is as basic as it gets. Similar to a boat trailer fender, a flat unit like this is perfect on a retro-styled bike.

6

7

8

8 There is a lot going on here. Look closely at the rear of the fender and you can see the lip that lets the LED taillight peek out. The fender itself has been molded to the frame since the bike is a rigid and movement with the suspension is not required.

9 A fender in name only, although it would keep the rider off the tire in case of emergency, this OCC spiderweb design became quite famous in the bike world.

10 Even bagger fenders can be custom. A few extra inches added on, a license plate shaped into the metal, and a really cool taillight give this fender bonus points.

9

10

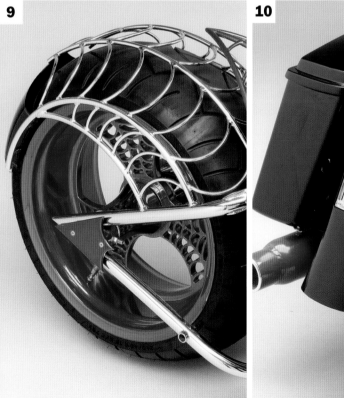

11

11 Not just a piece of metal wrapped around a tire—the extra length on the bottom and the tapered front piece represent hours and hours of metalwork.

12 And it is all steel. This Jim Nasi fender is big, round, and basically hides the entire tire. It took as many hours to shape this fender as it does for some people to assemble a whole kit bike.

12

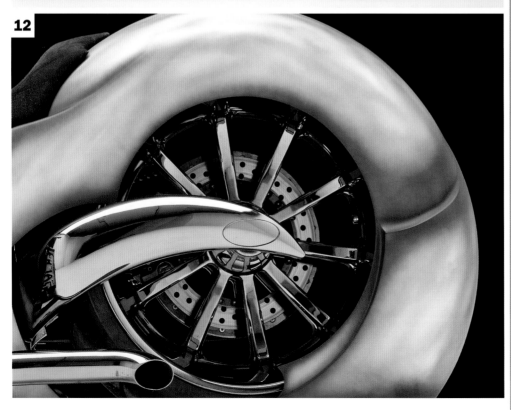

13 Look at how Donnie Smith made the fenders work on this bike. Even though they are vastly different in width, the lines front to rear are similar and the extra work putting the license plate and taillight in the rear unit keeps them looking like a smooth pair.

14 The big tires at both ends of this Exile bike almost mock the size of the fenders. Yet as you look at the bike they seem to present a commanding stance and add to the girth of the machine.

15

16

17

15 With a nice kick to the rear, this fender adds some dimension to the back of the bike. It's not so long as to be a worry when backing up to a curb, but accentuated enough to be custom.

16 Shown here is another sport-bike part that makes its way into the custom world. This fiberglass fender looks fast sitting still.

17 Reminiscent of the fenders on old Indians and Harleys, this wrapped front fender has a cool running light built in. Rather than trim away material to hide the springer mount, the full shape of the blank was used to add thickness to its look.

18 Making the most of the rear fender, Mondo built this one to provide all-weather protection, carry a taillight and license plate, and do double duty as a tie-down rack. Very cool.

19 Roland Sands used a Goodyear racing slick on the back of his bike for a racy look. He complemented it with a short, very aggressive-looking fender.

20 Things are not always what they seem. This rear fender on the Wakan Racer is also the gas tank and a place for the seat to mount.

18

19

20

21 When Kevin Alsop built his first sportbike, he used a fender panel that hugs, rather than adding an extension to keep debris off the gorgeous paint on the seat section.

22 Rick Fairless likes tie-dye paint. He added a new dimension to his rear fender by using heavy gauge screen to be the basis for the wild paint. Not much protection, but very unique.

22

23

23 By extending the frame horns back far enough, the rear fender gets a solid support mechanism, and some weight is saved eliminating extra fender struts.

24 This is a classic full fender offering plenty of protection and solid construction. Notice it has no visible fender struts.

25 If you think back to the fenders that used to be used on Schwinn Stingray bicycles, you will see a lot of similarity in this fender on Trevelen's chopper—lots of coverage and a tire-hugging profile that gets supported by the sissy bar.

26 Curved fender struts add movement to the back of this bike by Scott Long. The chrome also brings even more vibrancy to the green paint.

27 Multiple angles add plenty of dimensions to this Chica rear fender. By matching the same shape in the exhaust collector, the theme of the bike becomes obvious.

28 Earlier we talked about the importance of allowing for tire growth at speed. This Freddie Krugger design emphasizes just how important that is. If the tire were any closer to the taillight, it could rip it out at speed.

28

29 This curvaceous front fender is built by Jerry Covington. The flat bottom and the paint combine to add shape and dimension that isn't really there.

30 When the design allows, combining parts will add extra style to your bike. The curved fender struts on this long Ness fender are extended on the chain side to also be a guard. A clever idea that steps up the clean look of the bike.

31

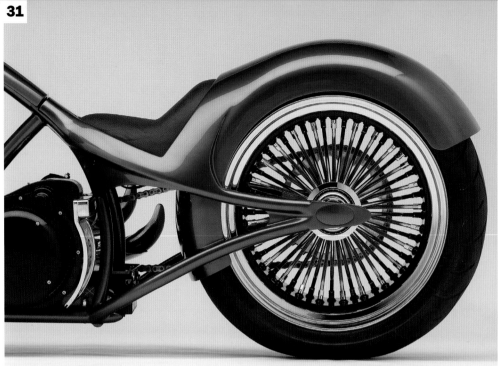

31 You know you did some nice bodywork when your fender seems to be a part of the frame, as this Sabers Specialties rear fender does.

32 By building the fender struts into the fender, Donnie Smith was able to carry the paint theme across with no interruptions.

33 A very cool trick is to mount the rear fender to the swingarm on a softail. Many builders attach the fender to a rigid, but doing it on a softail requires a lot more planning to assure the seat, frame tubes, and many other components can come into contact with it on full suspension extension.

32 **33**

34 There is a lot going on with this fender. It houses the taillight, seat bucket, and internal fender struts. Notice how the drop section around the taillight flares out for tire clearance on full-suspension collapse.

35 By mounting the fender with brackets that make it part of the springer, it can be set very close to the tire, and there is no concern with metal-to-rubber contact.

36 Why run a rear fender when you can build a one-piece fender/saddlebag section? To add a different touch, this tail section lifts up and away from the tire on gas-charged strut rods.

Gas and Oil Tanks

When you think about gas and oil tanks, your obvious thoughts turn to fluid containment. And while the tanks are clearly intended for fluid, short of the frame, nothing sets the tone for the look of the bike as the right—or wrong—gas and oil tanks will.

Tanks are made from steel, aluminum, and composite materials. Today, unlike 20-plus years ago, beautiful, flowing gas tanks—and oil tanks—can be bought right out of a catalog. These pre-made tanks can be the perfect solution to your bike planning. But even as pre-made, pressure-tested, internally sealed finished goods, there are still considerations you must take into account when you buy them.

Let's look at the basics first: fluid capacities. Most V-twins need between 3 and 4 quarts of oil to function properly. So if you are setting out on a journey to build your own oil tank, keep that capacity in mind. For those who are going to use the very cool idea of utilizing the lower frame tubes for an oil tank—again, keep capacity in mind.

Capacity carries over to the gas tank as well. If you are building a bike that you want to ride across country, a small, "peanut"-style 2-gallon tank is a mistake. Conversely, when building a stripped-down, bare-bones chopper that is as narrow as possible, a set of 6-gallon fat bob tanks may offer a bit too much capacity. So the key is to find the right combination of capacity and style for your bike.

1 Attention to detail from every angle. Notice how the filler panel under the gas tank gives it a flush mounting appearance.

2 By digging in deeper on the tunnel, Billy Aaron almost hides the fact that the frame has upward stretch in it.

3 While artistically beautiful and showing amazing craftsmanship, the actual fuel capacity of this tank is probably very small. Remember, anything below the fuel supply valve is lost.

4 A standard wraparound oil tank is accentuated with a filler panel that makes it appear almost twice as big. This is a great way to hide additional electronics or make way for a really wild paint scheme.

Don't assume all gas tanks end up on top of the frame. Many of today's top builders find creative placement for the fuel to reside and use the traditional tank area as a place to put such things as a battery, fuses, and air intakes. Look for fuel in a tank built in under the seat, in the frame, or even in the rear fender. Nothing is off-limits for the creativity of a tank except the basics of capacity. Let your imagination run wild as some of the builders featured in this section did.

5

6

7

5 By building the frame neck out with filler panels, the gas tank is made to look like a piece of the frame. Only when you see it from below can the mounting hardware be seen.

6 Looking more like an art deco sculpture than a gas tank, Billy Lane showed what creativity and focus on style can do for a bike with this gas tank.

7 Yup, that chrome barrel with the shifter reflecting in it is the oil tank. Simple and clean, it works really well on a chopper.

8

9

8 Remember: There are no rules when you build a bike. Who says you can't have a barrel oil and gas tank?

9 All too often, gas tanks are built with wild looks but barely offer any fuel capacity. Notice how deeply over the engine this tank drops—but it has a fuel supply valve at its lowest point to ensure all the fuel is used.

10 The oil tank is pretty standard here. But by building up the frame and fender to look like one piece, the oil tank becomes much more powerful in the design.

10

11

11 Gas or oil tank? Actually, it's both. Looking closely at the lower front portion of the tank shows one of the oil tank lines leading out—a styling trick that has been around for almost as long as there have been motorcycles.

12 Shown here is a peanut tank with recessed side panels. Building a tank like this is a lot of extra work, but it really gives such a small piece a lot of style.

12

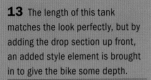

13 The length of this tank matches the look perfectly, but by adding the drop section up front, an added style element is brought in to give the bike some depth.

14 Back in the early 1970s, coffin tanks were really popular. Not so much today, but this modern version brings a smile to the face of many classic chopper fans.

15

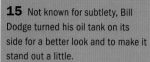

15 Not known for subtlety, Bill Dodge turned his oil tank on its side for a better look and to make it stand out a little.

16 Long, swoopy lines with sharp angles lead us back to the theme throughout this book: there are no rules.

16

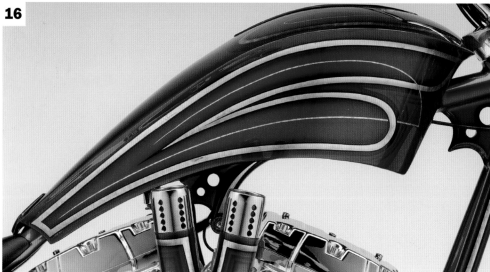

17

19

17 Sophisticated and beautiful, the tank is seemingly a piece of the whole bike. By crafting the tank and seat panel carefully, there is just a barely visible seam that separates the two.

18 What appears to be a standard Sportster tank is far from it. It has been given a flat bottom and a tall neck filler area. The flat bottom allows it to mount high on the frame rail for a more pronounced stance.

19 Big from any angle, the gas tank on Jim Nasi's bike is massive. But when you look at the rest of the bike's size, it blends in perfectly.

18

20

20 It's not just about slapping a barrel oil tank in place. It is really about making it the right tank for the bike. The huge barrel oil tank looks right on this bike and is fit to the primary plate perfectly.

21 Look closely at the frame on this bike, right near the front of the seat and just ahead of the exhaust pipe, and you will see oil lines connecting to the engine. The frame is the oil tank, which helps keep the bike looking minimalistic.

21

22 When is a tank not a tank? When it is an airbox cover like this one found on the Harley-Davidson V-Rod. Fuel is under the seat, but the shell shown here still is stylish.

23 Beneath the incredibly detailed leatherwork lies a regular steel gas tank. But the leather looks so much better than paint could.

24 This Walz hardcore bike takes split tanks to a new level. Each side is a fuel tank, connected by crossover lines under the pair. This system allows the tank to ride at frame level, lowering the profile of the bike.

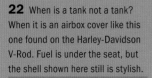

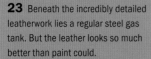

25

27

26

25 This small tank has a unique shape and looks cool high up on the frame. However, it was designed to make the most of it by positioning the filler up as high as possible, and the fuel supply valve sits low to drain all the fuel it has.

26 This aluminum fuel tank is gorgeous. No paint needed, just let the sun shine on the polished aluminum, and crowds will gather for hours.

27 Another case of something not being what you think it is. The fuel tank on the Wakan Racer is built into the rear fender. This cover holds the downdraft air intake and electronics.

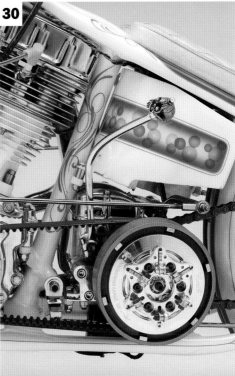

28 Guess where the oil tank is? A close look shows not much thought went into the placement, as the oil feed and return lines are coming right out of the front section of the gas tank.

29 A spun aluminum-barrel oil tank. Small, not flashy, and clearly supporting the racy style of the bike.

30 The most common oil tank for softail and rigid frames is the horseshoe tank. This one has been notched to allow clearance for the shift linkage.

31

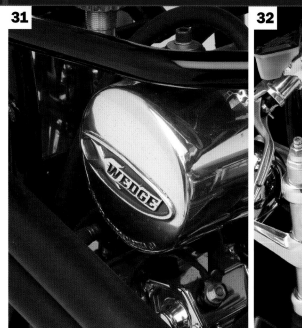

32

33

31 When your company is named Chopper Dave's Casting Company, making oil tanks that have cast-in logos is all in a day's—or week's—work.

32 Another Chopper Dave tank, this one was cast with fittings for the fuel line to create a fuel gauge.

33 The shape of the gas tank on this wild chopper built by Chica is enough cool for anyone. But by adding the oil tank—and building the oil-filler spout—to the top of the bike, Chica scores a homerun in cool points.

34

35

34 Is it art or a gas tank? Could be both, but in either case it shows the talent and perfection that went into this Dave Cook nickel-plated tank.

35 Another version of the traditional horseshoe tank, Jerry Covington added shape and dimension to the bottom with a sculpted-billet trim panel.

36 This swoopy gas tank by Zach Ness is complemented by the three levels of spike in the paint. Obviously the lower portion of the tank holds no fuel, but it looks great regardless.

37 It sure looks open and clean in the rear of this Bill Dodge bike. Look closely under the transmission, and you will see the hidden oil tank that allows for that open look.

36

37

38 Now *that* is a gas cap. When Keiji Kawakita of Hot Dock built this bike, he said if he sold it he would have to create an instruction manual for the gas cap.

39 When Donnie Smith built this gas tank, he decided that rather than use a dash panel, he would build one into the tank to add dimension and shape. The center fill design keeps the sides clean.

40 Look closely at the center of the downtubes on this Bourget Chopper. See that cap? It's the oil filler, since Bourget machines carry their oil in the frame.

41 Not only is the shape of this gas tank unique, it appears to be built into the frame. And it carries an electronic fuel pump to supply the fuel-injected engine.

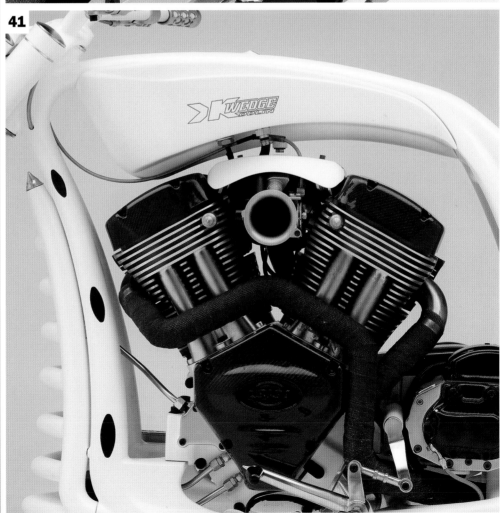

Seats

Deciding what seat to put on your custom bike is a big deal. Do you want comfort or do you want cool? In my experience with custom bikes, a seat is a make-it-or-break-it proposition. Go for the good looks of a sleek, low-profile seat and you are going to be miserable on that beautiful Sunday morning when you wake up wanting to knock out 500-plus miles. Go for the big pillow-top and it's awfully hard to win a bike show with your chopper. What is a builder to do?

Since a seat is usually held in with a front mounting tab and a set screw in the back, get both types of seat. Switching them out usually takes less than 1 minute and it gives you the best of both worlds.

Having ridden a rigid chopper with a seat made of a nice flat piece of sheet metal covered by a two-tone leather wrap for well over 200 unplanned miles, I am a believer in a comfortable seat. Many seat manufacturers have started working toward the perfect blend between style and comfort by replacing a portion of low-profile foam with a gel insert.

Seats have always been an additional area of expression on bikes (remember the king and queen seats of the 1970s?). The standard black leather gave way to metal flake vinyl and colors that blended in with the bike. By the early 1990s, seat makers were using multicolored leather to match a custom paint job, making the seat disappear in the scheme of the bike.

But in the past five years or so, the ante has been upped. Builders are now using rolled steel, shaped aluminum, and carbon fiber without

1 Kim Suter invested extra time when designing this seat to add the look of the paint into the leather. It also looks thick enough to make riding for more than a few blocks tolerable.

2 The seat and gas tank are shaped perfectly together. A small detail, but it really adds a lot of points when a judge looks at your bike in a show. Smooth matching lines look so much better than a big gap at the end of the seat.

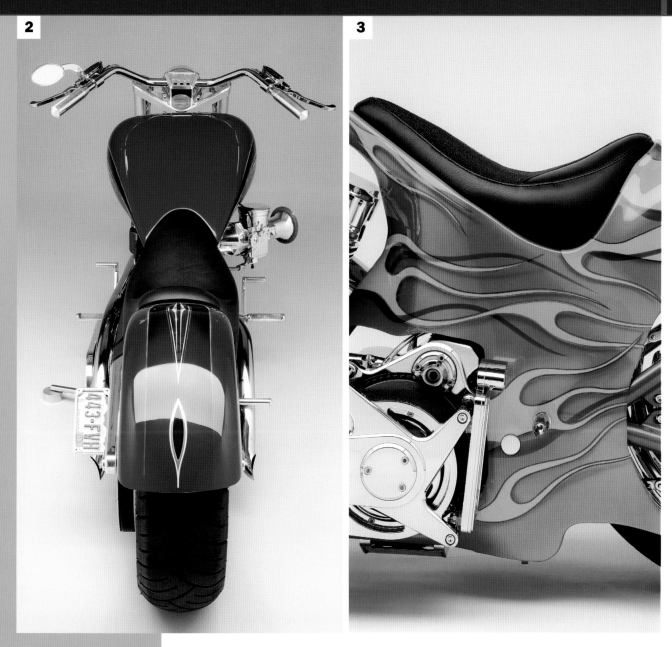

2

3

even using a simple leather cover and replicating the look of early board track racers. The intricacy of their work is so good it can stand uncovered, blending the style of yesterday with the high-tech fabrication of today.

One thing is for sure: A seat is the way to go. Romantic a notion as it is to have someone ride on your fender behind you, it just scratches your paint and leaves your passenger less than thrilled with the ride. A good seat can extend your ride, enhance your passenger's experience, and add much more riding time to your life.

4

5

6

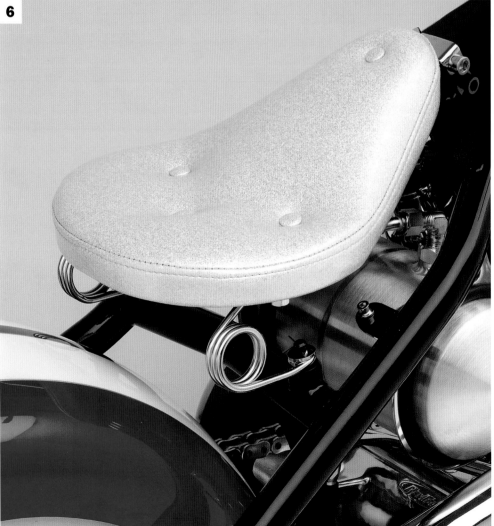

4 Although not the seat you want for a 1,000-mile day, this seat shows off what it looks like when a seat is made "tooled"—a process similar to a tattoo.

5 Not much more than a sheet of leather over steel, the springs underneath make the seat a little more comfortable. But it's clear that this seat was designed for form over function.

6 Not all seats have to be black. This seat cover makes the design blend into the bike style better and the springs add some comfort.

7 Sleek and stylish, this seat has stitching and multiple materials in its design. From the looks of it, the seat is held down by either Velcro or a suction cup. Hardware would make no sense.

8 A standard black leather seat was turned into a piece of art by adding stitching that matches the theme of the bike.

9 Attention to detail wherever possible makes all the difference. Picking up on the blue paint in the bike, blue stingray was worked into this seat to make it perfect for the bike.

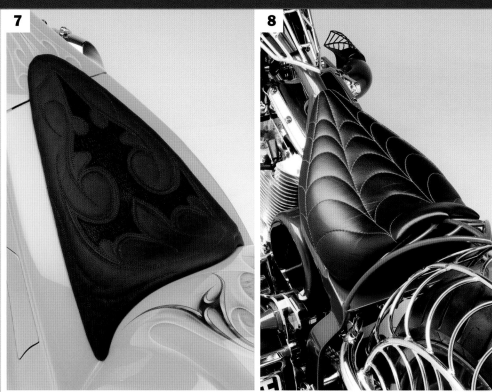

10

10 Another example of creativity in a seat; probably not very comfortable, but really well ventilated.

11 Clearly comfortable, yet really good looking: This bagger seat is a nice blend of all-day comfort with sleek lines.

11

12 When Paul Yaffe built this bike for Jeff Gordon, he built a seat that would be fairly comfortable and carried the number Gordon races with—another style trick for leather.

13 Sleek and small, this seat really blends into the lines of the bike—however, too much acceleration too quickly and you will slide off the back and hit the fender. A show seat for sure.

14 Everything you—and a passenger—could want in a seat can be found here. Plenty of space, decent padding, and a sissy bar for your passenger to relax on. Perfect.

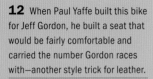

15 Cool. A drop-seat frame that really has a drop seat. It couldn't be any cleaner.

16 It could be a seat off a tractor, or it could be custom built. Regardless, it is good for holding you in place, but not the ultimate in comfort. By adding a small shock on the post, comfort is increased dramatically.

17 Balance is a good way to describe this seat. It has all the looks of a custom seat, has the shape to accentuate the bike, and has enough of a rise in the rear to keep you in place when you whack open the throttle.

18 A racy look is achieved by building the seat to fit into a one-piece surround that grows out of the frame. Walz Hardcore uses the seat to accentuate the flat red color and vents.

19 The seat is retro and modern, all at the same time. Jeff Wright from Church of Choppers built this seat to hold him firmly in place during aggressive riding and added the tail section to up the sporting qualities of his bike.

20 Krazy Horse Customs had no intentions of being comfortable on this seat, but they sure had a performance theme they could drive home.

18

19

20

21

21 To turn heads when people look at your seat, use alligator or crocodile. It may not make animal-rights groups happy, but the effect is eye catching.

22 Conventionalism be damned, Rick Fairless makes a statement with this seat.

22

23 Comfort for two—a king and queen seat.

24 By adding a small pad to the rear fender, comfort goes way up, as does the ability for this seat to hold the rider in place.

25 You can get away with a lot less padding on a seat if it has some give elsewhere. In this case, the dual shocks provide plenty of cushion over bumps and make the seat look lean and mean.

26

27

26 Not too much different in this seat, but the mounting brackets should spark a number of ideas for your bike. Simply drilling holes in an otherwise flat bracket gives a really nice look.

27 Sleek and clean, this little seat is good-looking. Probably not the best choice for cross-country riding, but for a Sunday putt it's alright.

28 The seat and tail section of Kris Krome's bike are all business. The added color panel in the seat is a nice extra.

29 Small details can make a big difference. Without the chrome grommets this would look like any other black seat, but with them it is show stopper!

30 Just because it's styled to blend in with the bike, doesn't mean it can't be comfortable. Donnie Smith does his seat right.

31

31 A combination seat. The front portion of the seat holds the rider in place while the passenger rides in plush comfort.

32 This Arlen Ness seat could be pretty comfortable—except for the gas and oil caps sticking up.

32

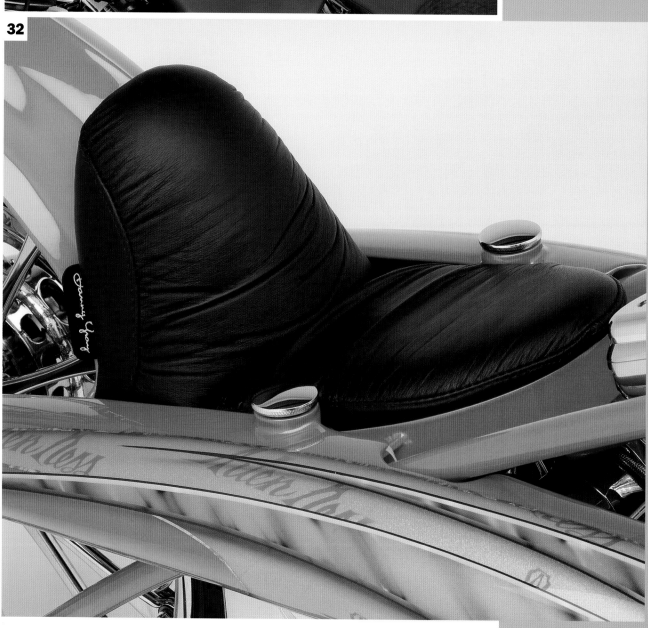

33

34

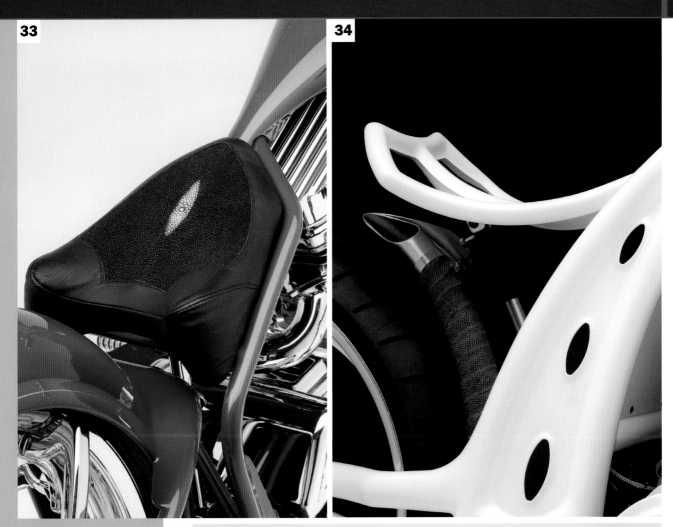

35

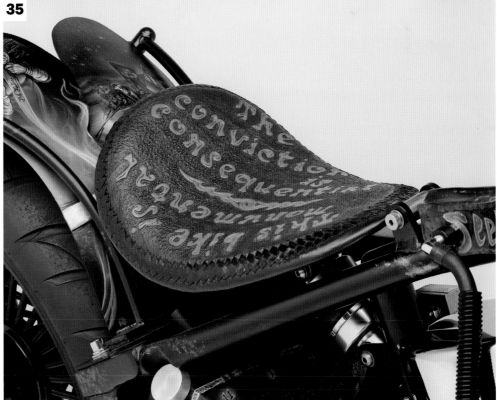

33 Cory Ness built his stingray seat to offer enough room to sit but still allow plenty of room for the fender/swingarm to move.

34 Again and again in this book I have said the limit is your imagination. This seat, metal and more metal, should be really uncomfortable, but the gas shock under it offers a bit more comfort than you might expect.

35 Any part of a bike can be a canvas to tell a story. David Anthony chose his seat.

1 As stripped-down as can be, this telescopic fork has had the legs "shaved." It means that all of the mounting tabs for brakes, fenders, and reflectors have been cut off.

Suspension

There is a big difference between the suspension of a daily rider and that of a custom bike. When you know you'll be hitting the road every day, you need a combination of ride comfort and suspension compliance to keep the tires on the ground, regardless of how many bumps you hit. On a custom show bike, ride quality is a distant second to the cool factor you need.

Looking at most custom bikes, you will find a minimal amount of suspension variety. Most customs are either rigid frames or softails. Very few use traditional-shock rear suspensions. So you will see springer, girder, and standard front forks with the occasional inverted unit thrown in up front.

Rear suspension has a pretty standard casting list as well. Rigid bikes will have no rear suspension by definition, and softails can have either conventional hydraulic shocks or air suspension. There is something cool about an on-board air compressor that allows you to lower the rear end of your bike when you park and inflate it when you are ready to leave. Not much variety for the custom crowd, but cross-country riding is rarely in their plans.

If you are customizing a stock bike, pay some attention to the suspension. If you lower it, look for a re-valve kit that offers more suspension compliance while giving you the lower look you are after. Don't cut shocks down. Instead, order a set that is calculated at the length you need. Remember: Decent suspension is the key to keeping your tires on the ground, and that's when you have traction.

2 Big and burly looking, this Goldammer fork assembly features a one-piece triple tree set and top fork cover. Expensive but beautiful, the style is unmistakable.

3 The inverted fork started on sportbikes, but when it transferred over to custom bikes it got really stylish. Tapered sleeves leading to the lower tubes really finish off a clean look.

5

6

4 Notice how low the rear of this bike sits. It seems like the fender would rub the tire if you tried to move—and it would. This bike features air suspension in the rear that inflates and deflates on command thanks to a hidden compressor.

5 Shown here is a traditional springer—with no extra anything.

6 Coil-over shock absorbers typically offer the best ride on a motorcycle's rear suspension. But when they are this short, don't expect them to be perfect.

7 The forks on this bike are extended enough that a fork brace was mounted in the center to ensure they don't flex in turns or in hard braking.

8 Shown here is a twist on a classic design, literally. Springers can be as wild as you want, and, as you can see, the whole bike reflects the twisted theme.

9

10

11

9 Telescopic forks don't have to be clunky and rough looking. Jerry Covington selected a set with beautiful lowers that taper and have a rounded finish. Notice how the fender mounts seem almost hidden on the inside of the leg.

10 A softail frame usually has a telltale sign that lets you know it is a softail and not a rigid—a pivot point. Notice the round cover over the pivot almost hidden behind the exhaust.

11 Not a conventional softail style—even though it looks to have the recognizable pivot—and certainly not a conventional rear swingarm and shock assembly, this mono-shock design is extremely eye-catching. By being so close to the pivot area of the swingarm, the shock can have minimal travel and still offer plenty of travel.

12 Shown here is a hybrid of girder and springer technology. This stylish fork design draws plenty of attention and makes people wonder how it works.

13 Another example of a Goldammer front end, this extended chopper fork accentuates the one-piece design of the triple trees and top sliders.

14 Talk about slammed—this bike has no kickstand. Instead, it has hydraulic and air suspension that can be lowered until the frame sits flat on the ground. Power up the electrical system, hit a switch, and it pumps back up.

15

16

17

15 This shiny chrome front end is a girder. Although rare these days, they were amazingly popular in the late 1960s and early 1970s.

16 When you see a front end this long, it will most likely be riding in raked triple trees to make sure the steering has proper rake and trail. Notice the exaggerated length of the bottom tree in relation to the top—that is what is meant by raked trees.

17 Shown here is a standard coil-over shock with plenty of travel. Hit a big pothole with a bike using these and you won't be cursing.

18 Modern sportbikes all seem to use this style of inverted front fork assembly. When you can work one into a custom V-twin it always looks cool.

19 Paul Cox used this girder fork on his creation to set the feel of the bike. Mean and purposeful, it really has a great look.

20 Jesse Rooke is probably the first builder to incorporate his own design single-side front suspension into a bike. It was also a shock to the custom world when it came out—especially as people had seen him ride it, so they knew it worked.

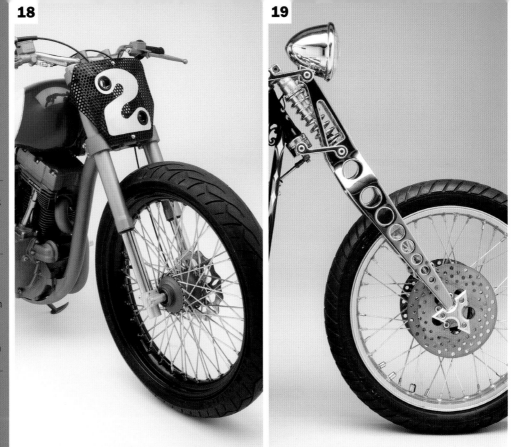

21

21 Race-ready, this Paul Beamish–built bike is a sporty race replica. The gold-anodized upper tubes are set off brilliantly by the highly polished billet triple trees.

22 Classic coil-over shocks are given an upgrade with remote nitrogen reservoirs. The remote unit allows the fluid to cool quicker, keeping the shock working better longer.

23 Stealing a few tricks from Honda, Skeeter Todd used this single shock to suspend the swingarm on his bike. By passing the swingarm around the shock, it can mount to give plenty of travel and a lower seat height.

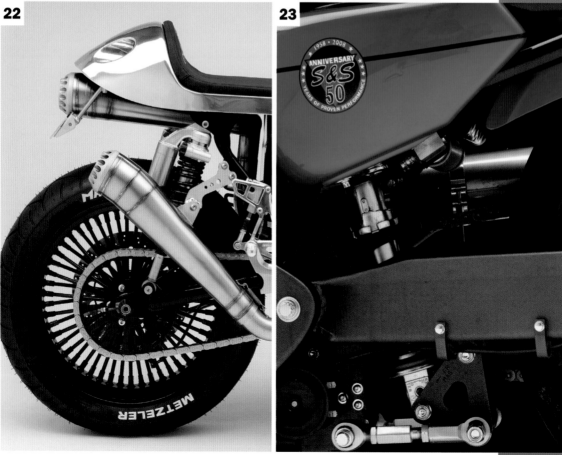

22

23

24 This girder fork designed by Kiwi Indian offers a smooth ride and plenty of travel.

25 Years ago, plunger-style rear suspension was pretty common. It worked better than having no suspension, but it wasn't really plush. Kiwi Indian puts a new twist on it with a fully dampened air shock taking the place of the plunger.

26

27

28

26 Not much to the fender on this Sucker Punch Sally bike, but notice how the fender mounts were used to create a little bit of extra fork bracing.

27 Chopper Dave added a very simple cool trick to basically stock forks to make them stand out: fork boots. Originally used by dirt-bike riders to prevent rocks from nicking the fork sliders and ripping out the seals, these simple black boots add a very cool touch.

28 Scott Long took the looks of his front suspension as serious as possible. The contrast between the beautiful chrome and the gold trim on the leaf springs goes a long way to make it stand out.

29 With a single shock connected to the swingarm, bumps can be a lot less annoying on this Dave Cook–built bike. Interestingly, the swingarm looks like a softail style but works like a conventional swingarm-style suspension.

30 Built by Freddie Krugger, this springer does triple duty by providing front suspension, incorporating the handlebars, and mounting the headlight.

31 A conventional coil-over shock with remote reservoir by Works Performance. Going the extra mile for a quality shock will offer a much better ride in all situations.

32 Another take on fork boots, these billet Covington pieces add the same look as the conventional black rubber pieces, but with a new level of style!

33 There is no rule against using cool, old bike parts to finish your custom. Bill Dodge used a fork from an old Hodaka dirt bike, with a nice coating of metalflake paint for some extra wild cool.

34 An extended inverted fork is really cool—especially when it is connected to a full fender and multi-spoke wheel.

35 This Kris Krome fork assembly is his unique creation. It features an elastic damper mechanism that offers a smooth ride and plenty of control.

36 Another look at a rear swing-arm design that looks like a softail but uses conventional shocks that compress on impact. A shock will always give a better ride when it compresses to absorb a bump rather than expand.

37

37 This short inverted fork uses triple trees with a little bit of machine work in them to add some style to an otherwise simple design.

38 This Ness chrome springer has built-in bars that are perfect for the bike. More than likely, Arlen had to rechrome the springer once he had the bars perfect, but it looks like it was worth it.

38

39 Not sure what to call it, but this single-side, dual-tube suspension was built by Fred Kodlin.

40 The round swingarm, finished in chrome, adds a sleek look to this standard swingarm-style rear end.

41 Look quickly at this fork assembly, and you might think it is one piece with no travel. Look closer, and you can see how the top section hugs the tubes so closely it creates the illusion.

Wheels

The only thing the wheels on a custom motorcycle have in common with any other motorcycle is that there are two of them. It doesn't matter whether it is a spoke wheel or a billet wheel—wrapped in rubber, these hoops are vital to the look of a bike.

The wheels of a custom bike are often the key to its style. More than a few builders machine their own wheels to create a starting point for a bike. Starting with a big chunk of

aluminum, they sometimes spend 80 to 100 hours carving the wheel that will draw your eye into their design and keep your focus between those wheels. If not, there are dozens of manufacturers that create gorgeous sculptures that will enhance the look of a bike.

Changing the wheels on a stock bike can make a dramatic change in the machine—a Fat Boy or Heritage that swaps the stock 16-inchers out for 18s looks incredible. Pitching

1 Todd Matteson spent as much time designing and machining these wheels as some people need to rebuild a bike. Plenty of engineering went into ensuring his safety. He rode this bike all over after he built it. Notice though, with this much open space in the wheel, how prominent the rotor becomes—even from the other side of the bike.

2 Soncy Road Speed and Custom knows that spokes sparkle in the sun. With this many spokes, the sun could blind you. Wheels with 100 and 120 spokes are an easy way to draw attention to a bike; the only problem is keeping them clean. Getting a polish rag in between all those spokes can be an all-day affair.

the 19- and 16-inch wheels on a Sportster and running a set of 18s can make the bike look aggressive and sporty.

However, you don't need to spend a fortune on wheels to change the look of your bike. Stock wheels laced with chrome spokes and a fresh coat of chrome or powdercoat on the rims can create an incredible transformation—at significantly less cost than new

wheels. This has been proven repeatedly in the past few years as the low-dollar bobber has come to its peak of popularity. Just a quick makeover on the wheels, please—direct the cash into something else.

Regardless of what direction you choose, the right wheel can completely change the look of a bike—and, of course, the wrong wheel can ruin it.

3

4

5

3 When Joe Martin wanted to build a bike with a truly aggressive stance, he knew the wheels would have to be part of the look. These dual-spoke wheels are aggressive, sporty, and definitely bring out the profile of the machine. This bike wouldn't look right with spoke wheels or solid wheels. The open space and sharp angles pick up on so much of the concept of the machine.

4 This seemingly stock bagger has the right wheels to set it off. Tossing the factory 16-inchers for gleaming billet 18s transformed the stance. Going a step further and timing the rotors (matching the rotor to the wheel) gives a completely custom look to a slightly modified stocker.

5 A basic bobber, as built by Brass Balls Bobbers, doesn't have to cost a lot to look cool. A chrome rim, spokes, and the right-size tire give a bike the period-correct look the designer was after without breaking the bank and pushing this bike beyond affordability.

6 Notice the wheels? Billy Lane certainly wasn't going for low key when he put these billet wheels on his bike. With the lines of this chopper, Billy could have used spoked wheels and gone for a look that became part of the bike, but by using these proud, in-your-face wheels, he gave his bike a radical, exciting look.

7 Shown here is a springer connected to a spoke wheel with a drum brake. This is as classic a style combination as you will ever see. exciting look.

8 Seem like this wheel is missing something? Billy Lane shocked the world when he did the hubless wheel. A sophisticated bearing system lets it roll and supports it on the swingarm connection.

9 How would you like to clean this wheel after a ride in the rain? The wheel builder laced this wheel to accentuate the pattern of the spokes following each other—rather than traditional crossing of the spokes.

10 Clean and exciting, the rear wheel in this photo looks like it is freewheeling. Actually, this bike has a caliper and rotor mounted on the output shaft of the transmission and the tire is driven by a friction drive. Slick, custom, and not for everyday riding.

6

7

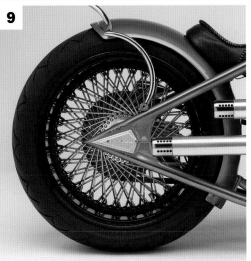

8

9

10

11

12

11 A tremendous amount of design work went into this wheel to ensure it would be strong enough while still having the spiderweb look designed into this OCC creation.

12 Looks pretty busy back here, doesn't it? With right-side drive and a right-side caliper and rotor, the left side of this wheel is wide open and clean. Actually, this side looks pretty high tech.

13 Sometimes a wheel can be a central style element of a bike. The wheels on Jeff Gordon's Paul Yaffe–built chopper were engineered to have his number in their design.

13

14

14 Wheels don't always have to match to look right on a bike. With knobby tires, the mixed wheel seems like the right choice.

15 No front brake? Yes there is. Inside the hub is a brake with two pads that make 360-degree contact with a minirotor (so to speak) when hydraulically activated. It stops and it looks cool.

16

17

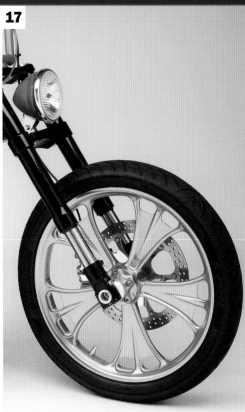

16 A very simple way to add a really custom look to your bike: Use wheels and rotors with the same pattern cut into them. The look of a matched package is hard to beat.

17 Adding color to a wheel can make a huge difference in how it looks on a bike. The gold really complements the black fork.

18 Straight off a race bike, this polished three-spoke wheel is aggressive and bold. Adapting styles from another type of bike can really add a new dimension to your custom.

18

19 The mounting point for this Walz Hardcore wheel appears to be a knock-off hub, just like the old Ferrari race cars it is built to praise. The look is stunning and really complements the black wheel.

20 Spoke wheels with a huge dual-action drum brake may not be the most modern piece on the planet, but the look is tremendously retro cool.

21

22

23

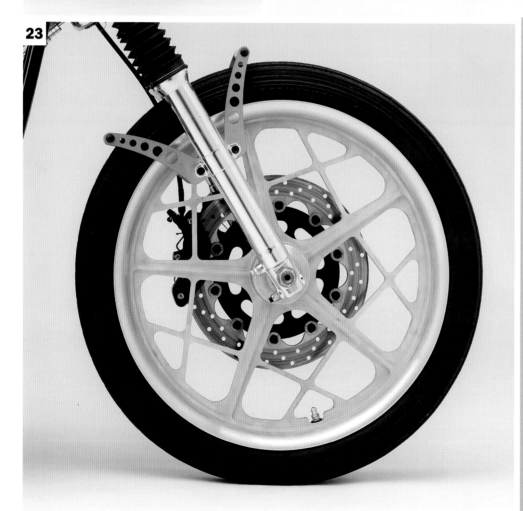

21 This is a look you won't see on every bike: black rims and spokes with racing calipers and radial tires. Sportiness is conveyed. Classic café racer style is maintained.

22 Back in the early 1970s a set of five-spoke Invader wheels was the coolest accessory you could buy. Finding a set now is almost impossible.

23 Inspired by the BMX (bicycle motorcross) bikes of his youth, Chopper Dave worked with Jeff Wright to create these wild-looking wheels.

24 Chica makes reproduction-style Invader wheels. In this case, he incorporated an old H-D drum brake to add a really retro look to his wheel.

25 The bigger the rotor, the better the stopping power. Dave Cook uses a perimeter design rotor to allow a smaller caliper to have plenty of surface area to clamp down on.

26

27

28

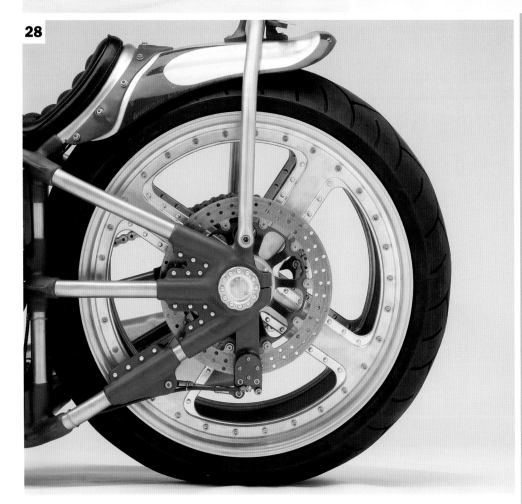

26 They call matching the rotor and sprocket of your bike to the wheels "timing" them. As you can see here, the effect helps the sprocket almost disappear and makes the wheel look that much better.

27 These bold spokes resemble dog bones. The classic contrast of the black rim and the chrome spoke is visually strong and just unusual enough to grab extra attention.

28 Bold and stocky looking, these wheels were handmade in the shop at Hot Dock in Japan. The builder is such a perfectionist, all of the Allen-head bolt positions line up.

29

30

29 Spokes can be bold and prominent. This Sabers Specialties wheel looks even nicer thanks to the two-tone rim.

30 A few years ago there could never have been a wheel like this, but advances in the machining world have allowed the seemingly round lip to be manufactured easily. The contrast of the lip and the angular spokes makes this a great-looking wheel.

31 It's not often you see a whitewall tire on a chopper, but this one looks right, especially on the spoke wheel.

31

32

33

32 When you run a fat tire—250, 280, 300, 330, or 360mm—and you put the drive and brake on one side, you end up with a deep-dish wheel like this.

33 Everything in this picture—except the tire, rotor, and caliper—is made from carbon fiber. That means the wheel, swingarm, and fender are all lighter than any aluminum part, and stronger too.

34 Cory Ness took a complete reversal on wheel design here. A wide hub, narrow rim, and three-dimensional spokes create a look like no other.

34

35 Notice anything missing on this wheel? How about a belt or chain and brake system? Fred Kodlin uses a friction drive to move the tire and a transmission disc brake to stop it for a super-clean look.

36 Another example of timing your wheel and rotor. You really have to look closely for the rotor's carrier spokes.

37 Detail can make all the difference in a wheel's look. The use of chrome nipples on the black spokes and rims make these wheels gorgeous.

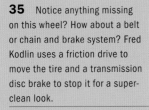

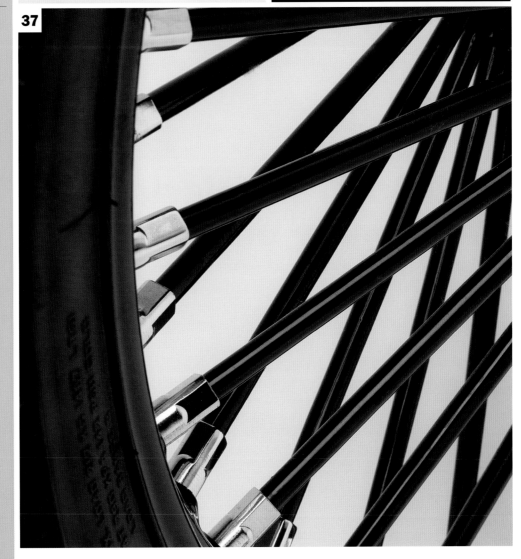

Engines, Transmissions, and Primary Drives

For the most part, all V-twin engines look the same. The cylinders are spread 45 degrees apart, there are two pushrod tubes on each cylinder, and a carburetor sits proudly between the heads. But beneath the basic cosmetic similarities lie unique styles of engineering. Each manufacturer has its own idea of what makes the engine perform best.

While almost all of the bikes in this book have 45-degree engines, they have many different designs. There are Knuckleheads, named because their rocker boxes vaguely resemble the knuckles in your fist.

Then there is the Panhead, again based on rocker boxes that look like, well, pans. Shovelhead, likewise. The most common style of engine is the Evolution. Its rocker boxes are just square pieces of billet, so the engine name came from its revolutionary all-aluminum design. The latest version of the 45-degree engine is called a Twin Cam, very similar in design to the Evolution but with two cams and a new oiling system.

Transmissions all basically look the same: a cast or billet case filled with gears. In the mid-1990s, rear tires started getting big—200mm-plus on

1 The engine is polished to a brilliant shine. The fins at the base of the cylinder have been shaved off—it adds a very high-end look but it does compromise cooling abilities. On a show bike you can get away with it. Notice how the brake arm bracket and the cam cover work together.

2 Classic beauty. An open-billet primary makes a bike look tough and cool.

up to 360mm now—and the right-side drive option became a necessity on big twins. Left- or right-side drive is probably the only visible difference when you look at a transmission, but internally they can be dramatically different. Some transmissions have all-helical gears; some are half-helical and half-standard; some have four, five, six, and seven speeds.

These two components are connected by a primary drive. Custom bikes feature unique primary drives since the primary is a way to show off styling ability, design, and engineering. The most common is the standard chain-in-oil primary enclosed in a sealed case. Next would be the belt drive—designed in open, closed, and semiclosed versions. Then the customized primary comes into play—

open-chain, belt-drive designs that incorporate other components like oil filters, regulators, ignitions, or whatever the imagination allows.

Combine the three and you have the heart and soul of a bike. How big the heart is, well, that's up to you. V-twins can be as small as 45 cubic inches and up to 1,454 cubic inches. That means horsepower can range from about 35 all the way up to 200! The choice of how much horsepower can be a big factor in deciding what you use for a transmission and primary—200 horsepower is going to require a pretty stout system! Regardless of what you choose for power, the combination will set the tone for everything about your bike, so spend some time studying the options.

3

4

3 An old trick to add a custom touch to a bike without adding a tremendous cost factor is to paint or powdercoat the cylinders. If you are going to powdercoat, remember to do so before you fit the pistons as the powdercoating process heats the parts up to about 400 degrees Fahrenheit. That is enough to distort the bore.

4 Polish an engine enough and it starts to look less like an engine and more like jewelry. The upswept carbs with downdraft velocity stacks add a cool touch.

5 Two things to talk about here. The primary cover is called a "tin" primary. Typically found on older Panheads and Shovelheads, it is the classic cool look. The big cover on the back of the primary is called a derby cover—because it vaguely resembled a derby back then. Today they don't look the same, but the name continues on.

5

6 Some belt-drive primary assemblies can be pretty wide. Karata has been making 4- and 5-inch drives for years. Look closely and you can see the chrome transmission top cover and a very polished case.

7 The transmission end cover is made by P.M. and it indicates a hydraulic clutch. If you have not thought of using a hydraulic clutch, rethink things. Smooth operation, no cable to adjust, and extra cool points.

8 This Sportster engine has been painted red to add some cool styling. You can always spot a Sportster—or XL—engine by the very small primary cover. Since the transmission is built into the case it can be much shorter, enabling a Sporty to have a shorter, better-handling chassis.

9

10

11

12

9 The combination of short, wrapped exhausts and the forward-mounted velocity stack make this S&S Evolution-style engine look pretty fast even in a picture.

10 This is a Knucklehead. Far from stock, this one is wearing plenty of show bike polish and chrome. Still, when you look at the rocker boxes, you can tell what it is.

11 On a Twin Cam–powered bike, the engine and transmission are bolted together for added strength. It's an easy way to tell if the bike you are looking at is a Twin Cam or not.

12 And then, sometimes, just to mess with people, a builder puts something like this together. The front cylinder has a Shovelhead rocker box. The rear is a Panhead. Wild stuff when you add in the dual carbs and the magneto.

13

13 The primary cover in this photo would be the normal closed-style primary, but this one is open and run dry. Just above the case is the Pingel air-shifter, which tells you the bike is meant to go fast.

14 A good example of creativity: This bike has an open chain primary and a hand shift right off the gas tank.

15 For the most part, when you see a Panhead, the rocker covers are chrome. This builder went to a very cool satin finish on all the would-be polished or shiny surfaces. A modern-retro look is achieved with minimal extra cost.

14

15

16

17

18

16 As you look at the profile of this little rigid machine, it exemplifies the term "bare-bones." The open belt drive is simple, no extra billet covers, the hand shift barely reaches the seat, and the foot clutch is low key to complement the look.

17 Yes, that is a cool-looking open belt drive with nice billet accessories. Notice anything missing though? The bike has no belt or chain driving the rear wheel—instead, a friction drive coves off the transmission output and rubs against the back tire to "drive" it. Very cool, but not really an ideal way to run up the mileage.

18 Many people call the Panhead the most beautiful engine ever. Add billet rocker covers and a *billet cam cover* and it reaches up even one more notch in the cool department.

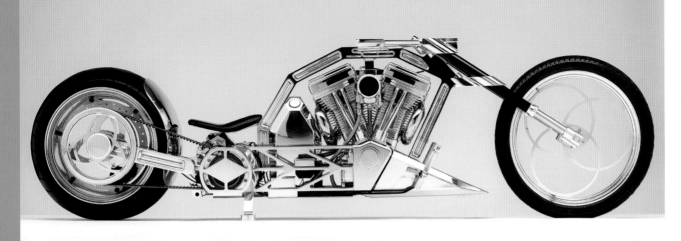

19 Earlier in this chapter I spoke about the engine, transmission, and primary being the heart and soul of the bike. There is no doubt about it when you look at this radical machine. The billet frame is amazingly cool, but the drive train gives this bike life.

20 Unbelievably cool, and almost nonexistent these days, a Flathead engine makes a bike stand out in a crowd.

21 Not all belt drives have to be huge to be cool. This narrow belt drive allows plenty more cornering clearance on the left side and still adds a muscle element to the bike.

22

23

24

22 Another tin primary, this one runs as an open unit with a very chromed derby cover to add some cool.

23 That is a supercharger—a very easy way to add a huge shot of extra horsepower to your engine. By pressurizing the intake pressure well above atmospheric pressure, more power is on tap as soon as you twist the throttle. Of course, if you add a supercharger, be sure to add a heavier clutch, primary, and well-set-up transmission.

24 Massive fin packs and a 56-degree spread makes the X-Wedge stand out from the crowd. Fuel injectors mount directly in the heads, three cams hide under the big chrome cover, and Ferrari red paint dresses this engine up.

25 Another shot of the AQG bike. This really emphasizes how the paint helps the style of the engine. Also notice how the primary is a mix of polished components and industrial standard finish for a beefy look.

26 This Twin Cam engine was treated to carbon fiber coverings on the rocker boxes and cam cover. The effect screams performance. Another interesting item is the routing of the pipes to the other side of the bike, leaving the engine out in plain sight.

27 Church of Choppers-approved, this Shovelhead engine is ready to run. The magneto comes straight out of the timing cover, forcing the brake lever to be replaced with a thumb lever under the left handgrip. The air cleaner has been modified to provide more flow.

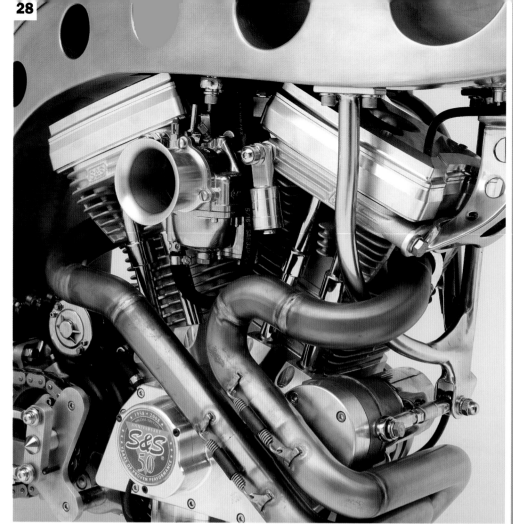

28 This Sportster-style 100-cu-bic-inch S&S engine seems to float in space. It is a stressed member, providing support to the frame and eliminating the lower cradle.

29 The exhaust on the Wakan Racer is designed to provide maximum ground clearance and performance. Oversize silencers make sure you can get away with going fast without drawing a lot of attention.

29

30 Looking at this S&S X-Wedge engine, it's clearly bigger than most. A neat extra on this is an exhaust that crosses behind the rear cylinder in an X pattern as a complement to the engine itself.

31 A tin primary and a standard-look Shovelhead. The chrome, natural aluminum, and black finishes look perfect together. Sometimes stock works.

32 When old meets new, the result is gorgeous. Trevelen took this Panhead engine from S&S and added billet rocker boxes, white paint, and a whole lot of polishing.

33 Chopper Dave was the first builder to do any custom work with an X-Wedge. Since the cams are driven by a dry belt, Dave was able to cut the cam cover open and simulate an "open belt drive" on his engine.

34 Classic beauty, the Panhead with almost no modifications. In the case of this S&S version, the timer cup holds a 12-volt electronic ignition, and the oil pump is a much more powerful version than the original Panhead used.

35 Open belt drives are very cool looking, so are open chain drives, but the chain lacks lubrication running that way. This Baker closed-chain primary still has an open area for cool, while allowing the chain to ride in oil as it was designed to do.

36 A very wild Shovelhead built by Dave Cook. The rocker boxes and cam cover have a very custom look, a nickel finish against wrinkle black paint.

37 The velocity stack coming off the S&S D-series carb and the unrestricted exhaust are not necessarily what you want on a street bike. But this package is on a land-speed bike, and making noise is all part of the fun!

38 Plenty of detail and nothing ignored is the theme behind this Covington-done Shovelhead.

39 Sometimes less is more—especially in the case of this Ness belt drive. Simple covers, no outer supports or brackets, and a nice chrome backing plate let the overall look stand strong with no clutter.

39

40 Anodizing billet parts can be a durable method of adding color to your engine. Bill Dodge did that on this Shovelhead, and the result is fantastic. Of course dual magnetos don't hurt either.

41 They do it differently in Japan. The builder of this bike, Hot Dock, created his own mechanical fuel injection for this Shovelhead. I have never seen anything like it.

42 A little gold trim and some
blue paint make this Panhead
sparkle. It doesn't take a lot. In fact
just a small amount of contrast can
really change an engine's look.

44

43 The backside of a 145-cubic-inch Evolution engine. One of the biggest engines around, the 145 is capable of close to 200 horsepower. Notice the extra length in the cylinders and the taller deck on the cases.

44 The heart of Zach Johnson's bagger is a 126-cubic-inch Twin Cam engine that uses a radical two-into-one exhaust that has no baffles or restrictors—perfect for quarter miles or touring with earplugs, of course.

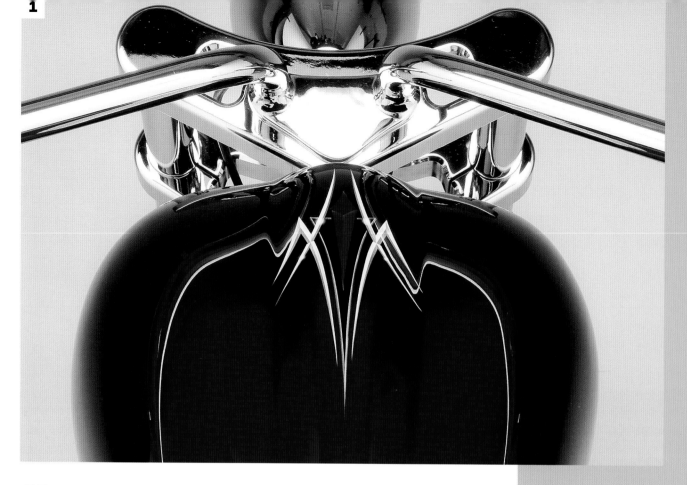

1

Handlebars and Controls

To some, handlebars are handle-bars. They come with a motor-cycle and owners never even think about changing them. Many people don't know that changing handle-bars can completely change the way you ride a motorcycle. Your posture, comfort, and attitude are really dic-tated by how you hang your arms.

Handlebars do not need to be store-bought, either. Making handlebars is not really that hard, and making your own will allow them to blend into the design of the bike even further. If you decide to make your own bars, put some extra effort into ensuring that they are strong enough to handle all of your weight slamming into them as you hit a pothole—because it can happen. Also, remember that if you

plan to use a conventional handle-bar clamp to hold them in place, you really should knurl the area that will fit in the clamps to give them a bit of extra bite. If you don't have a knurl-ing tool, you can simulate the same effect by using a center punch and hammer to dimple the area that will be clamped.

Controls are obviously a big part of handlebar design. Will you have brake and clutch levers or twist-style controls? Will you have brake or clutch controls on the bars at all? What about switches for lights and starting? How will you run the lines and cables and wires? Plenty of deci-sions to be made before you settle on a set of bars.

And then there are foot controls and hand shifting. Many custom bikes run

1 By building the handlebars into the top triple tree, Mark Warrick cleaned up the top lines of his front end a lot. Notice how clean the welds are around the bars, adding a nice element of style.

2

a jockey shift with a foot clutch and a lever coming up from the transmission for shifting—almost all of these are handmade to complement the style of the bike. Every so often a builder will incorporate a clutch lever into the shift arm, making it a one-limb operation.

I mentioned twist controls earlier. In case you don't know it, there are a number of kits on the market that will allow you to have a clutch in the left grip that you twist like a throttle to actuate. Very clean in design, it adds plenty of cool to the bike. Another cleanup trick for a custom bike is to build a brake system that is linked—meaning the operation of one lever actuates the brakes at both ends of the bike—which is usually done through the back brake to keep the handlebars clean.

A last word on controls: Try to match the style of the hand and foot controls so they create a nice flow through the bike. Sleek, nonobtrusive hand controls and huge, clunky foot controls on the same bike won't help you win any trophies.

2 Don Watkins knows what I was saying about matching controls. Notice the hand and foot controls have the same style—pretty modern looking—and how he chose a handlebar clamp that added to the look.

3 They call them drag bars: short, flat, and forcing the rider into an aggressive riding position. Kendall Johnson usually builds huge-horsepower bikes, so drag bars complement the style.

3

4

4 Joe Martin built his handlebars as part of the bike. They're unique in using a hydraulic clutch so that the hand controls match side to side. By using hydraulics on both sides he can run the lines in the bars for a much cleaner look.

5 For this Tempest Cycles–built bike, pointy things were a theme. To accentuate the style, notice how the footpeg, shift lever, and handgrip all come to a point. The clutch lever is missing because the grip rotates to activate the clutch.

6 David Molina really went for a wild approach on his bike. A Hurst-style automotive shifter is positioned on the right side and he operates his clutch with his left foot—not a setup for entry-level riders!

5

6

7 Tom Langton uses clip-on handlebars to add a performance feel to his bike. They work perfectly for the style of bike and complement the massive inverted fork tubes. Both the hand and foot controls are made by the same manufacturer, Performance Machine, ensuring a nice match.

8 When you can't find anyone who makes what you want, make it yourself. Indian Larry tried to make most of the parts on his bikes, adding originality and extra class. The shift lever on this bike is a perfect example.

9 Um, yeah. Well, Dan Cheeseman is not afraid to try things that are different. From the upside-down, reverse-mounted handlebars to the wild, mile-high shifter with a clutch lever built in—his bars and controls are radical.

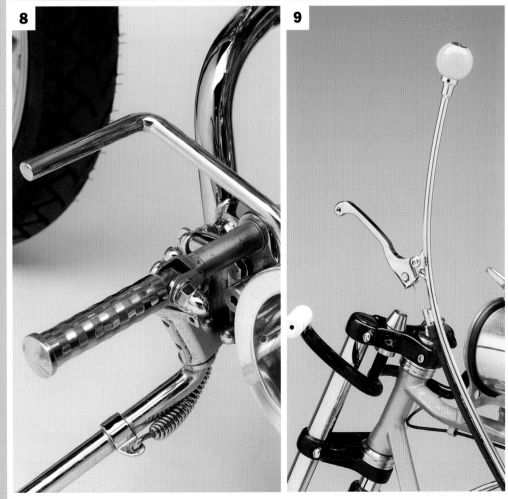

10

10 They call them mini-apes because they are a smaller version of traditional ape-hangers. These, on a Sucker Punch Sally–built bike, are perfect for the profile of the machine. An internal throttle keeps the bars looking Schwinn Stingray clean.

11 Don't feel, even for a minute, that you are limited to the manufacturer's finish choices. You probably can't buy red anodized controls out of a catalog, but Eric Gorges wanted to go the extra step on his bike and it added a great look.

12 Stretching up to the sky, these ape-hangers will sit you up very tall on your seat. Landmark Custom Cycle used an internal hydraulic clutch line to add extra cleanliness to their build.

11

12

13 Rudy Chappelle seemed to keep building up on his chopper. Notice the very tall handlebar risers and the mini-apes are complemented by an equally tall shift arm coming up beside the gas tank.

14 Minimalism at its finest. Jesse Rooke has always embodied a bicycle style into his bikes and this shows just how seriously he takes it. The bars are devoid of any visible controls—or clamps for that matter—and the foot controls match perfectly.

15 By seeing all of this bike you can understand how important handlebar choice is. Jesse Jurrens built his Low-Life chassis to be long and lean for a stretched-out profile. Use of any other style of handlebar would make the ride incredibly uncomfortable.

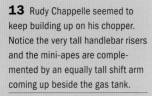

16

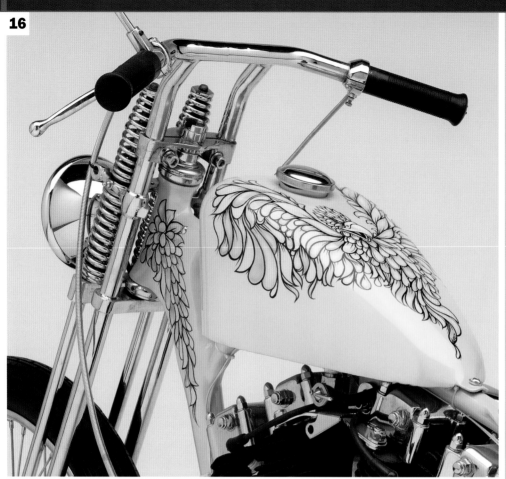

16 One of Arlen Ness' first custom bikes, the handlebars seem to grow out of the Springer. Simple back hand grips and a throttle and clutch were the cleanest you could do back in the late 1960s and early 1970s.

17 Can you find the hidden handlebars in this photo? Aaron Greene went with form over function on this design, putting his handlebars way out of reach—but the look seems perfect for this bike. Aggressive and hard-edged, the bars will force Greene to hold on tight when the supercharger kicks in.

17

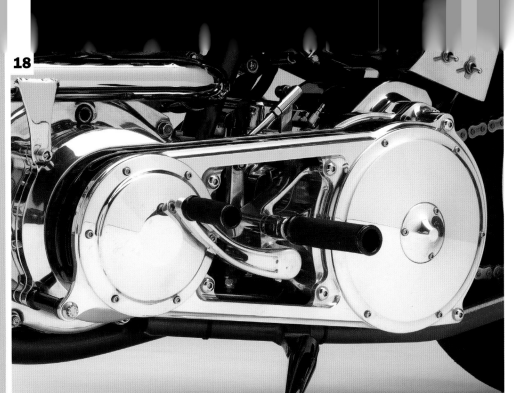

18 Because forward controls are not always the answer, Chica used a set of midcontrols inside an open belt drive: a unique look and a great idea for those with shorter inseams.

19 With a little bit of everything to show, Roland Sands makes quite a statement with his handlebars and controls. Custom-styled bars with sharp angles and a reverse curve at their base, midcontrols with a foot clutch, and a very cool shift lever; convention is thrown out the window.

20

20 Now these are some big handlebars. Set to follow the angle of the springer, and rich with curves and shape, Jerry Stephenson went the extra mile with an internal clutch line for a sanitary look. A clutch cable would have just flapped in the wind in this design.

21 Definitely one-off, Billy Lane added a special twist to his shift lever. Hand grips and footpegs of the same design tie things together.

22 Borrowing heavily from the automotive world, Z Cycles built some pretty cool controls for their bike. A billet floorboard shaped like a 1970s gas pedal and a B&M Shifter with a line-lock on it take you back to a muscle car of days gone by.

21

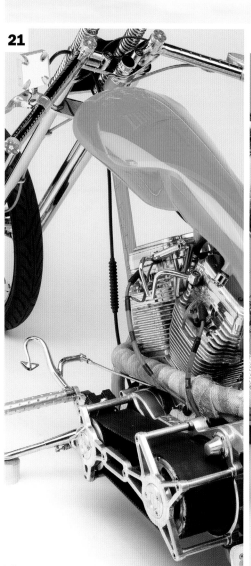

22

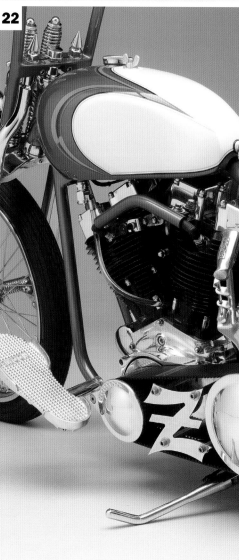

23 Swooping shapes and aggressively knurled billet grips combine to scream performance. The billet controls and powdercoat bars are super clean thanks to hydraulic lines and an internal throttle placed within the bars.

24 The true definition of a clip-on handlebar. Mounted under the triple tree, short, and to the point, these bars are phenomenal when in a racing situation.

25 Pegs and controls mounted like this are called rear-sets. Used on sportbikes, they allow the rider to position his boot well above the road when leaned over while still being able to access the shifter or brake.

23

24

25

26

27

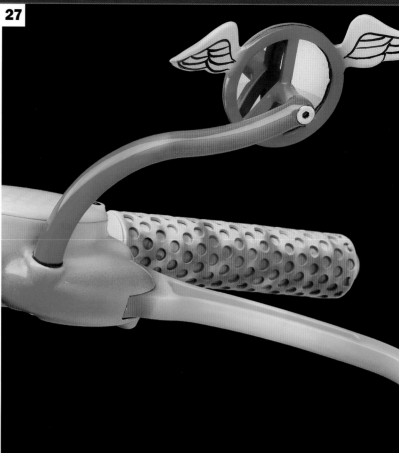

28

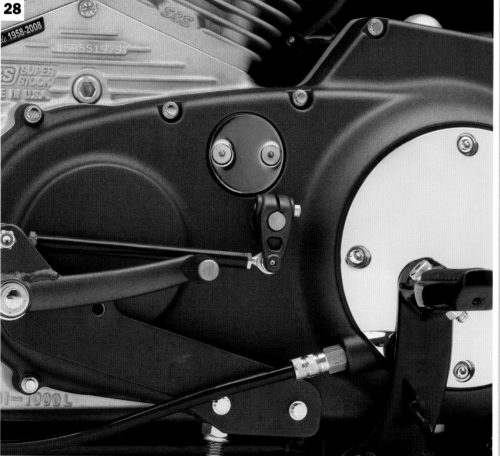

26 A classic drag bar look. These flat bars pull the rider forward for an aggressive position. Notice this shot also shows off a dual-belt drive incorporated in this OCC bike.

27 The limits on your bike are those created by your imagination. If you want painted controls that match your bike, go for it.

28 A little innovation goes a long way. To get slightly rear-mounted mid-controls, Skeeter Todd used a bit of Buell engineering on his shifter and combined it with his own bracket design to position his shifter exactly where he wants it.

29 This angle is about the only way to show how the handlebars of Chris Olson's retro chopper are built into his front end. A look like this requires careful ergonomic planning to make it work.

30 Designed specifically for this bike, Trevelen used 12-inch straight risers to hold the bars up where he wanted them. The simple white grips and only a throttle cable sticking out make things really clean.

31 Rather than splay the rider's feet out in the wind, this bike was built with mid-controls that tuck the rider's feet in tight to the bike and offer better control in quick-maneuvering situations.

32 Reverse levers are not a new idea but are rarely incorporated in today's bikes. Dave Cook goes a step further in the retro world with a wrapped grip.

33 Don't do a quick glance at this footpeg and shifter. Take a moment, and you realize that the plated pieces rotate around the actual wrapped footpeg to allow the unit to shift.

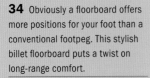

34 Obviously a floorboard offers more positions for your foot than a conventional footpeg. This stylish billet floorboard puts a twist on long-range comfort.

35 A key element in building a cool bike is consistency throughout the design. Clearly all of the trim and finish pieces on this bike were built to match and carry the theme. Additionally, by running internal lines the handlebars stand out more because they are uncluttered.

36 Mid-controls are becoming more popular every day. These Bill Dodge controls make the primary side of this bike.

37 Don't want rubber, don't want leather, but do want a different looking grip? Try jewels like Branko did with these turquoise grips.

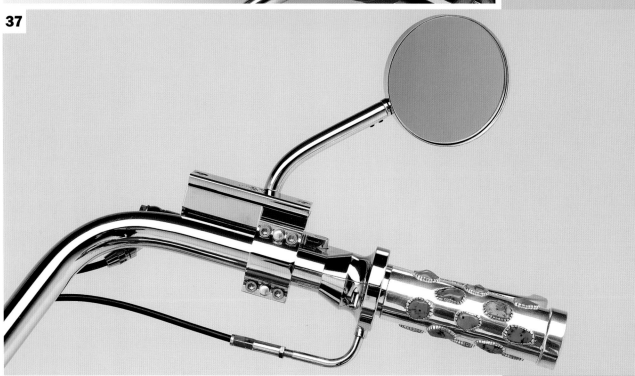

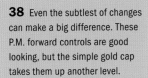

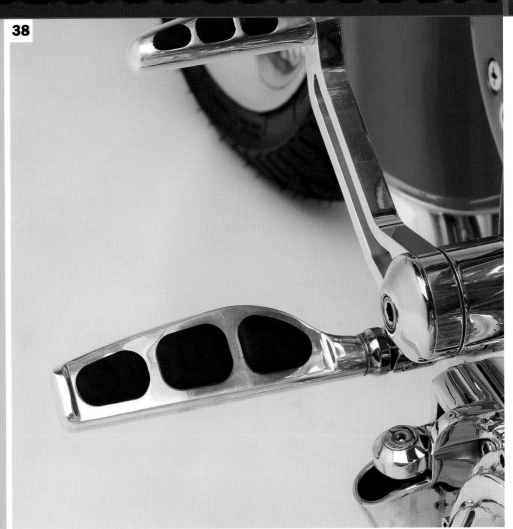

38 Even the subtlest of changes can make a big difference. These P.M. forward controls are good looking, but the simple gold cap takes them up another level.

39 Drag bars, a Super D carburetor, and two big exhaust pipes give the impression of serious performance when you look at it from this angle.

40 These bars have extra rise in the center, but drop back down in the grip area. The style allows for hidden bolt installation through the triple tree.

41 The best way to describe this footpeg and brake lever is three-dimensional. I really like the way the lever pivots on the footpeg shaft.

42 This Hogtech control uses internal linkages to operate the remote master cylinder for the rear brake.

43 Rather than mount a clutch pedal on the forward control, a lever is incorporated into the shifter to make shifting a one-hand operation.

Paint

Where does one start in discussing paint for a custom motorcycle? From solid colors to wild graphics designs, paint can dominate the look of a motorcycle. Some of the best painters in the world can command upwards of $10,000 to do a custom paint scheme, while other bikes have been painted with $27 worth of spray paint from a can and won shows.

Styles of paint can range from extensive airbrushing that can rival the work of the best tattoo artist to realistic flames to anything else you can imagine. Gold leaf, pin striping, flat and satin finish, chunky metalflake, and simulated granite are only some of the unusual styles of paint available.

How far do you want to go with paint? Will you bring the colors onto the frame and go for the whole package, or will you run a black frame that lets you change the paint scheme again and again? Part of the decision on the frame will depend on if you are building a ground-up bike or working from a stocker; stock frames are black 99 percent of the time. In order to paint it, you will need to remove every part connected to it, so the engine and trans, suspension, wiring harness, fork cups, swingarm bushings, everything must come off. Then once it is completely torn down, you can strip the factory coating off the frame—clearly a lot of work if you are not going for the complete show-bike look.

Back to the paint discussion, please take your time with this decision. Just because a paint style is cool today doesn't mean you will like it five years from now. And five years is not too long to expect

1 This Big Bear Choppers machine looks right with the two-tone paint. Adding a level of sport to the bike, the color choice accentuates the gold and black trim.

2 The flames in this OCC bike create an almost 3D effect. A checkered flag effect adds a nod to performance.

3 Really cool paint doesn't have to be loud. The subtle pinstripe that separates the blue and back of this design is classy and attention getting.

4 The original metalflake paint was big, thick, and chunky—just like this.

to keep a paint job with the costs associated with the process. Again, as stated earlier, many great-looking bikes have been painted with spray cans for very little money. However, there was still plenty of

prep time associated with the work.

Rather than spend a lot of time talking about what could be, let's look at some examples of paint work from all over the world and see what can be learned.

5

6

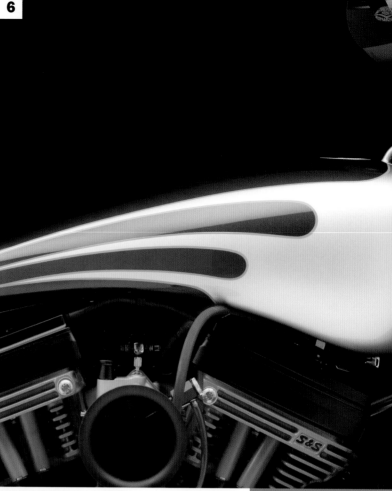

7

5 Another example of 1970s-period paint styles. A little bit of everything mixes together to remind you of how cool it was when painters started doing these techniques.

6 A simple scallop paint scheme is enhanced with a contrasting pinstripe between the colors.

7 Here is an interesting paint effect on Zach Ness' bike. It looks like this is a black-and-white photo, but it is not. Zach focused on using black, grey, and chrome on his bike, but no colors. It works.

8 Multiple colors and shades, chunky metalflake, and floating numbers make this paint scheme a winner.

9 Incorporating photos into the paint work of his bike, Branko was able to convey the theme of the S&S 50th Anniversary build and have a stand-out design.

10 You can't go wrong with old-style hot rod pin striping.

11

11 Paint is easily upgraded to look even better with raised logos that extend the length of this gas tank.

12 Airbrush art is, well, an art. The candy red paint over the black almost-tattoo-looking graphics is beautiful.

12

13 Sometimes paint is not paint at all. This Bourget Bike Works bike is coated with the same stuff you line a pickup truck bed with, makes for a cool look. Just be sure you really want it that way.

14 Back in the day, gold leaf was the hot ticket. In a bike just recently built, Cory Ness ties the old gold-leaf style with really modern candy colors.

15 Things are not always what they seem. The silver separation between the two colors on this bike is not really a chain, but the numbers 5 and 0 repeated over and over. The wild effect was part of a bike built by Dougz Custom Paint and Fabrication.

13

14

15

16

17

18

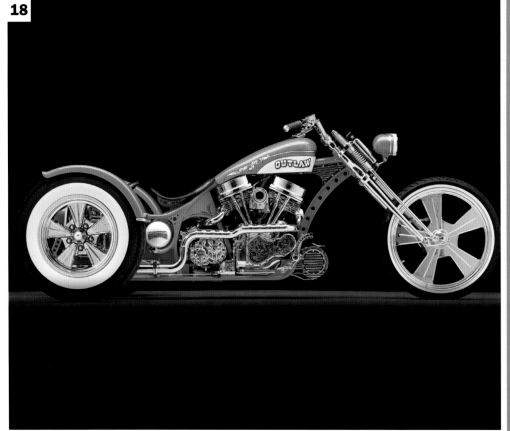

16 The message is in the cartoonish look of the paint on David Anthony's bike. Looking the whole bike over from top to bottom it appears to be the pages of an underground comic telling the story of struggle in America. Wild.

17 There is probably not a color in the rainbow that didn't make it into this Rick Fairless tribute to Janis Joplin. Bringing the wild tie-dye style onto so many surfaces of the bike—wheels, cylinders, handlebars, wheel pulley, and spring—meant a lot of planning and preparation. Well worth it for this wild look.

18 This subtle blue color actually enhances the radical look of Jerry Covington's trike. By adding silver leaf trim and a contrasting white panel that picks up on the whitewall ties, the whole package flows together.

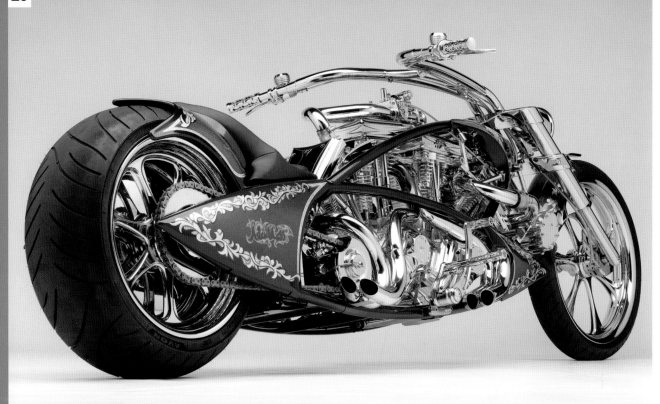

19 Even with a minimal amount of surface area, Arlen Ness was able to create a complex look in his paint. The base metalflake is accentuated with gold leaf and airbrush patterns.

20 Sometimes paint isn't really paint. Russell Mitchell used a carbon fiber wrap on the areas that would have been painted to complement the simple black paint he put all over the rest of the bike.

22

21 Bill Dodge took a simple approach to a very cool bike. By nickel-plating the frame he made it possible for a small tank and shirt rear fender to really stand out on the bike. He took an extra step to tie the design together by using silver accents in the tank and fenders.

22 Remember that comment in the introduction to this chapter about keeping a paint job for five years? Brian Klock shows the best way to be happy with paint for a long time: Pick a color you like a lot and use it everywhere, with no additional graphics. This simple red paint with a few black accents is a classic look that you can love for a long time.

23 No one has ever accused Eddie Trotta of being subtle, and this bike proves that. A base of tortured skulls over a block wall with chains and tribal graphics all combine to make a menacing package. Notice how the detail is carried to every piece of the bike. Nothing is overlooked to save a few minutes or dollars.

24 Classics never go out of style. This beautiful restoration done by Arrgo Conley shows just how good a simple two-tone paint scheme can look. The chrome trim found in between the black and red all over the bike was a functional styling element of the 1940s: Use the trim to allow for less-than-perfect seams between the colors.

25 Kendall Johnson relied on some serious airbrush work to bring this nightmare to life. Starting with a warm orange base color, Johnson brought skulls, bones, guns, axes, tribal graphics, and flames all into one design—not for the faint of heart or fans of rainbows and puppies!

23

24

25

26

26 Hard to beat tribal flames for grabbing attention. Kim Suter used a contrasting light blue with a fine pinstripe to make his tribal style jump off the deep blue basecoat. As you can see, taking the design onto the frame really adds some extra flash.

27 Many people in the custom bike world call Dave Perewitz the King of Flames. Looking at these classic hot rod flames over a deep red paint scheme, it's easy to see how Dave got that title. Look closely at how Perewitz added a modern touch by surrounding the flames with a contrasting blue.

27

28 David Molina took an interesting approach to a basic black bike by doing his frame in gray. Should he ever want to change the look of his bike, a simple paint job on the gas and oil tanks and rear fender would create new-looking bike.

29 Arlen Ness used a simple double-scallop pattern to make this green bagger jump off the page. Color choice can bring as much attention as wild graphics, and the vibrant green he chose allows the subtle graphics to look more complex.

30 Orange County Choppers knows a thing or two about making a bike grab attention. By bringing color to many areas that you wouldn't expect, they took their bike to a new level. Look closely at how they alternated the color on the cylinders. I know I would have liked to see that work being done.

31 The black frame on this bike, put together by Clair Glantz, accentuates the soft colors of the airbrush work. Another thing it does is allow Glantz to redo the sheet metal on the bike and turn it into a whole new machine by just painting two fenders and the gas and oil tanks.

32 Normally a two-tone paint scheme is a great way to achieve an elegant look easily. By adding in colorful graphics panels on the gas tank sides, Mondo Porras gave his paint design an edge in a bike show.

31

32

33 Taking a theme as far as it can go is exemplified by Pauline and Robert Brown. Patriotism and the flag design is evident everywhere, even in the seat that has been re-covered to keep the look flowing.

34 Proving that paint doesn't have to be shiny and new looking, this chopper built by Hogtech features flat paint and worn edges. While even a casual onlooker will know that the paint isn't really decades old, the extra effort makes this a cool design.

34

Index